The 100 Best Trees and Shrubs

A PRACTICAL ENCYCLOPEDIA

The 100 Best Trees and Shrubs

A PRACTICAL ENCYCLOPEDIA

PREVIOUSLY PUBLISHED AS PART OF *THE 400 BEST GARDEN PLANTS*

Elvin McDonald

RANDOM HOUSE · NEW YORK

A Packaged Goods Incorporated Book

Published in the United States by
Random House, Inc.
201 E. 50th Street
New York, NY 10022

Conceived and produced by
Packaged Goods Incorporated
276 Fifth Avenue, New York, NY 10001
A Quarto Company

Text and photography by Elvin McDonald
Designed by Yasuo Kubota, Kubota & Bender

Library of Congress Cataloging-in-Publication Data
The 100 best trees and shrubs: a practical encyclopedia
Elvin McDonald.

p. cm.

Includes index.
ISBN 0-679-76030-X
1. Plants, Ornamental—Encyclopedias. 2. Plants,
Ornamental—Pictorial works. 3. Gardening—
Encyclopedias. 4. Gardening—Pictorial works.
I. Title. II. Title: The one hundred best trees and shrubs.
III. Title: A practical encyclopedia.

SB407.M26 1995
35.9— dc20 94-35385

Random House website address: http://www.randomhouse.com/
Color separations by Hong Kong Scanner Arts Int'l Ltd.
Printed and bound in Singapore by Khai Wah-Ferco Pte. Ltd.
98765432
First Edition

Acknowledgments

Dedicated to Marta Hallett

Thanks to the home team, pals, and friends, particularly:

Kristen Schilo, editor; Mary Forsell, copyeditor;
Sarah Krall, assistant editor; Yasuo Kubota, designer;
Tatiana Ginsberg, production manager; Amy Detjen,
assistant production editor; Catherine San Filippo,
proofreader; Lillien Waller, helping hand; Carla Glasser, agent;
Douglas Askew, research; Tom Osborn, driver/gardener;
Rosalind Creasy, focalizer; James R. Bailey, neighbor;
Janis Blackschleger, telekineticist; Diane Ofner,
gardening student; JoAnn Trial, scientist, and Don Trial,
teacher; R. Michael Lee, architect; Charles Gulick,
gardener; Michael Berryhill, poet; Linda Starr, head
coach; Hila Paldi, body coach; Mark Inabnit, Publisher
and Editor-in-Chief, *Houston Life*; David Walker,
Editorial Director, *Houston Life*; Catherine Beason, angel
unaware; Maria Moss, Executive Editor, *Houston Life*;
David Warren, artist/gardenmaker; Audrey Scachnow,
tweak expressionist; Christy Barthelme, envisionary; Tino
and Richard, Stark Cleaning Services; Tony Williams, yard
man; Dan Twyman, pruner; and Leslie Williams, cheering.

Elvin McDonald
Houston, Texas
January 1, 1997

Contents

Introduction

The one hundred plants that appear in these colorful pages represent my pick of the crop as a lifelong gardener and horticultural journalist. They are far from being the only "best" plants. Some vast families and categories certainly deserve more attention. Most assuredly, I am already growing the plants and assembling the photography for a sequel. One of the most wonderful aspects of gardening is that we can never know all of the plants. For this reason, dedicated gardeners will always experience the thrill of the hunt, the excitement upon discovering a flower or plant more beguiling than could have been imagined.

How to Read an Entry

Within this book, plants appear in alphabetical order by botanical genus name. If you know only the plant's common name, look for it in the Index. The botanical name and its suggested pronunciation are followed by the common name or names, many of which are interchangeable, and then by the plant's family name, appearing first in botanical Latin and finally in English. For example, plants of the genus *Berberis* (botanical name) are commonly referred to as barberry (common name). They are members of the Berberidaceae (botanical family name), or barberry family (common family name).

Within the entries, species names sometimes appear, where applicable. For instance, in the *Callicarpa*, or beautyberry, entry, the species names *C. americana* and *C. dichotoma* appear. Both are broadly referred to as beautyberry. Oftentimes, species do not have common names and, as a result, are known in the plant trade only by their botanical names.

In all, one hundred different plants are pictured in this volume, yet many more are actually named, a resource unto itself for tracking down worthwhile species and cultivars.

Within each entry, there is also a guide for cultivation:

Height/habit: Despite the inexactness of horticulture and botanical differences, I sum up here as much as can be said about a genus in as few words as possible.

Leaves: Many plants are appreciated for their foliage as much as—or even more so—than their flowers. Here I provide a succinct description of leaf shapes and characteristics.

Flowers: Dimensions, arrangement, and color and fragrance characteristics are noted.

Season: The plant's high season appears here.

When to plant: I have used the phrase "Set out transplants when available" for nearly all plants in the book. In other words, if a gardener shops regularly for plants, both through mail order and locally (at nurseries, garden centers, and plant auctions held by public gardens), they will be delivered or sold at approximately the correct planting time for that person's hardiness zone. Containerization, lightweight growing mediums, remarkably efficient distribution, and computerization have revolutionized the plant business. Yes, there are still plants shipped at the wrong time and local retailers who sell inappropriate choices, but on the whole, the system works.

I have also provided each plant's tolerance for cold and heat according to zone, as appears on the United States Department of Agriculture's Plant Hardiness Zone Map (see page 112). (This information can also appear under "Season," if applicable.) However, please note that the U.S.D.A. map has traditionally been based on cold tolerance, not heat. Now the billion-dollar gardening industry is working to generate maps and zone awareness for heat as well as cold, also taking into account the relative dryness or wetness of a particular climate. To establish heat tolerance zones for this book, I have used a variety of references, including the catalogs of Louisiana Nursery, Wayside Gardens, and Yucca Do Nursery (see Resources). I have also consulted the books listed in the Bibliography, especially *A Garden Book for Houston* and *Hortica*. When in doubt, ask a neighbor who gardens for details about your hardiness zone. There are lots of variables and a host of gardeners who like nothing better than trying to succeed with a plant that is not rated for their zone.

Light: To prosper, most plants need strong light or some sun, in a site that affords air movement. Here, I provide specific light or shade requirements.

Soil: Most plants need well-drained soil that is kept evenly moist to on the dry side. There are rainy seasons when gardens are wet for long periods of time. If water stands for more than a few hours in your yard, this does not bode well for gardening—unless you are undertaking a water or bog garden. There are also dry seasons, and gardeners today generally subscribe to the concept of Xeriscaping: not to set in motion any garden that will require undue irrigation during normal times of drought.

Fertilizer: Generally speaking, 5-10-5 and 15-30-15 are good for flowering-fruiting plants. Timed-release 14-14-14 is an all-purpose, long-serving (up to a whole season from one application) fertilizer for a wide variety of plants. For acid-loving plants, choose 30-10-10 or chelated iron. Careful, consistent application of these or entirely organic fertilizers will result in vigorous growth.

Pruning: Instructions in this section are as specific as possible. Pruning is best learned by observing someone who is knowledgeable and then by practicing. If you select the right tool, never squeeze the handles until all your fingers are accounted for, and never do it when you're angry. Pruning is not only therapeutic for plants, it also benefits the gardener, as a way of generating discipline and instilling a sense of order in outdoor chores.

Propagation: Lots of gardeners favor propagation over just about everything else done in the course of a gardening season. It is fun to see little seeds sprout and roots take hold from brown-looking cuttings. It is also practical if you have elaborate plantings in mind.

Uses: Under this heading, each plant's strong points are discussed, though you the gardener may find your own unique usages.

As much as I can provide detailed information about the art of gardening, you will be your own best teacher, a philosophy stated most eloquently in this old garden verse:

> *If you seek answers,*
> *leave your questions*
> *outside the garden gate.*

Elvin McDonald
Houston, Texas   January 1, 1997

Chapter One

The Woody Plant Garden

ithin this grouping are the major plants used in making beautiful yards, gardens, and parks. Grouped together under the heading of woody plants, they all actually produce wood and have buds that survive above ground during the winter months. These plants give us shade and shelter, while also offering the ornamental value of beautiful flowers, showy or edible fruits, and exquisite varieties of foliage. Even when they are relatively short-lived, trees and shrubs stay around for at least a couple of decades.

Planning and Designing the Woody Plant Garden

Since woody plants may not mature for several years, they are often the first elements added to a new landscape. From the outset, the gardener should consider if there will be headroom for a tree or shrub as it matures, as well as if its roots could spread to encroach upon walls, foundations, and paving. Chapter Two indicates the mature height and width of each plant and facilitates landscape design with the future in mind.

The right tree or shrub in the right place will require little pruning and no extraordinary amount of irrigation during normal times of drought. Thorny types—such as barberry, rose, and pyracantha—are best reserved for barrier or perimeter plantings and are not practical choices near walkways or other places where there is heavy foot traffic.

Many homes have foundation plantings that look tidy at first—but without rigorous pruning and knowing management, they soon grow up to hide the walls and hang over the windows, casting a pall throughout the home. This is not to say that all foundation plantings are wrong, only to suggest that in many situations the house would look better with clean space all around and the usual front yard plantings moved to the perimeter of the yard. It then becomes possible to create flower gardens between the dwelling and the property lines, to turn these once-public spaces into private retreats. Consider, too, that planting deciduous trees on the east and west sides of your house gives you sun-filtering shade in summer while allowing light in during the winter.

All kinds of hedge and screen plants are also contained within the woody class, and these are included here along with trees and shrubs. Some can be as low as 1 foot (30 centimeters) high, while others tower at 12 feet (3.6 meters). They can be clipped into precise shapes or left to grow into natural shapes.

Nothing adds so much to the visual impact of a woody plant or ground cover as using it in multiples rather than dotted about here and there. Instead of a few ground-hugging evergreens for coloring in under trees and shrubs or in shaded areas where nothing else will grow, consider using just about any tree or shrub in this way by repeating them en masse over a sizable area to create a thicket.

On large or rural properties, mixed hedges or windbreaks up to 50 feet (15 meters) wide by many times as long are an excellent choice. These act as safe havens for wildlife and provide gardeners and flower arrangers with an endless source of delight.

Mixed shrubbery borders have great potential in large and small spaces, in city gardens as well as those in the country. If you wish to have four seasons of visual interest, make a detailed plan using graph paper, using each square to represent a given amount of space on your lot. Factor in the approximate space needed for each shrub you wish to grow. Also consider the light needs for each plant. The International Society of Arboriculture recommends planting the tree at a distance of half its height from houses or other structures.

Another option is planting a single specimen of tree lining both sides of a walk or driveway to create an allée. These can serve as giant hedges through which one can walk or drive, thus adding certain grandeur and even mystery to surprisingly small parcels of land.

Soil Preparation

Since woody plants by nature take time to become established and reach maturity, it makes sense to start them off with well-prepared soil. Almost all of them do best on a well-drained site; numerous kinds appreciate a constant supply of water and therefore thrive by the side of a stream or pond. These are noted in the individual plant discussions in the chapter that follows.

It is wise to spend more time making sure the endemic soil and any added to the planting hole mesh with the original container soil. Toward this end, the rootball of a container plant usually needs some pruning, perhaps slashing with a knife several times up the sides or pulling out the rootball with both hands from the bottom—a kind of filleting process. This helps the roots spread out into the new soil.

To further amend the soil, add a sprinkling of timed-release fertilizer pellets, such as 14-14-14, into the planting hole— even organic gardeners admit to doing this at planting time.

Buying and Planting Woody Plants

A practical approach to buying woody plants is to purchase container specimens on a regular basis from local nurseries and garden centers, always selecting plants just coming into bloom or showing colorful berries. After a couple of years of buying and planting regularly, the border will begin to move smoothly from one season to another, with no significant lapses when nothing looks promising.

Botanic gardens and arboretums are an important source for worthwhile, often unusual woody plants. If there is one in your area, inquire about membership and how you can participate in any distribution of worthy plants. Specialty mail-order nurseries are another impressive source for the best in woody plants; the names and addresses for some are listed in the Resources section of this book.

For many woody plants, which for simplicity's sake will be referred to in this section as trees, you'll have a choice of three different types: container-grown, balled-and-burlapped (B&B), and bare root. (B&B trees are increasingly rare at nurseries nowadays, however.) Before buying, make sure the trunks are relatively strong and capable of fully supporting the plant once in the ground. In overall shape, the tree should be well balanced. For bare-root trees, look for uniform, hearty growth emanating from all areas around the main root. If you opt for a B&B tree, make sure that the roots are not upsurging from the rootball, which indicates that they are too tightly packed. The rootball should be firm and compact.

When purchasing container-grown trees, the same applies: check to see that the roots are not circling the surface of the container or coming out of the drainage holes. Containers generally range from 3 to 5 gallons (11.4 to

19 liters), though some are larger.

When planting, remember that your hole should be twice or three times as wide as the original rootball. As far as depth is concerned, it is almost never advisable to set a woody plant more deeply into the ground than it was growing previously in the container. Dig the planting hole deeply enough so that the plant is at about the same depth, or slightly higher, than it was growing originally.

With bare-root trees, place the roots in the hole and fan them out. When planting a B&B tree, if it's encased in actual burlap cloth, leave it in place and simply remove the ties (if the "burlap" is another material that will not decompose, remove it). With container-grown trees, remove the tree from the container in the same way that you might remove a cake from a pan. Trim off any gnarled roots and place in the hole.

Then refill the hole and water. A great many trees are drought-tolerant after they become established; but early after planting, deep, slow watering is essential to their taking hold in a strong, reassuring way.

Sowing seeds, taking cuttings, layering, and dividing are some of the ways to propagate trees, shrubs, and ground covers. Seeds may or may not produce offspring exactly like the plant from which they were harvested. In the directions for individual plants in the chapter that follows, unless otherwise noted, instructions for sowing seeds are intended for outdoors, usually in some sort of protected seed frame. A frame allows the gardener to maintain evenly moist soil and to distinguish easily between desired seedlings and weeds. The seeds of woody plants from temperate zones often require a period of chilling before they can sprout, which is why fall and winter are often the recommended planting times.

Cuttings yield new plants exactly like the parent from which they were taken. Those made in the spring and early summer are often referred to as softwood and green wood; those from midsummer into early fall are called half-ripe and semiripe. Hardwood cuttings taken in fall and winter work especially well for deciduous species. It is beneficial to reduce the size of larger leaves by one-half to two-thirds so that the cutting has less top growth to support while it is establishing a set of roots.

Another way to produce new plants exactly like the parent is by layering, which usually takes place in early spring. The process is simple. It can be done by pulling a branch down toward the ground until it can be buried with at least one or two sets of leaf nodes below the soil surface. The leafy tip should stick out of the ground. Place a brick or rock on top to hold everything in place. Rooting occurs in one season, after which you can sever the new plant from the parent and transplant it.

Air-layering is a slight variation on this process whereby the gardener wraps a handful of moist sphagnum moss around a set of leaf nodes of a branch and then seals the moss and branch with plastic. This procedure usually commences in late spring after leaf development. After several weeks or months, new roots will grow into the moss. At this time—often as late as fall—the plant can be severed and transplanted.

Professionals, as well as home orchardists, use bud grafts to propagate new cultivars. This activity takes place in winter through early spring and involves inserting a bud on stock and allowing them to grow as one. A complicated process, it is not recommended for amateurs.

Caring for Woody Plants
Throughout the Seasons

This plant group is remarkably carefree on any given day. Low ground covers often can benefit from tidying up and removing large leaves and windblown trash. If there is a serious drought, any water that can possibly be spared should go toward saving the woody plants perceived as most valuable or the most difficult to replace.

Most woody plants benefit from an organic mulch 2 to 4 inches (5 to 10 centimeters) deep over their root run, which saves water, moderates soil-root temperatures, and reduces the number of weeds that must be pulled.

Inspect large trees regularly, especially after windstorms, to be sure all branches are intact.

Many experts recommend pruning in late winter through early spring, as trees heal more quickly at this time of year. However, some trees, such as oaks and honey locusts, do not respond well to pruning at this time of year; if in doubt, consult with your local nursery. The purpose of pruning is to remove damaged or dead limbs and branches that weaken the healthy parts of the tree and to shape the growth of the tree. Make angled, precise cuts.

Essential Tools

A shovel, not to mention a strong back, are necessary to dig planting holes. Another basic is a pair of sharp pruners with by-pass blades, for cutting wood up to pencil thickness; long-handled pruners or loppers, for cutting growth up to .5 inch (1.25 centimeters) in diameter; and a pruning saw, for branches up to 3 to 4 inches (7.5 to 10 centimeters) in diameter. Larger projects may require a power chain saw or the hired services of a professional.

Hedges are most ideally clipped with hand-powered shears, but most gardeners don't have the time or strength and prefer to use electric- or gasoline-powered hedge trimmers.

Year-round Gardening Calendar

Use this season-by-season calendar to organize your gardening schedule for woody plants.

SPRING:

At the beginning of the growing season, apply a fertilizer.

Begin watering whenever soil feels dry at a few inches down. When you do water, water well.

Before new leaves are out, inspect dormant branches for signs of scale insects. If detected, spray using a dormant or horticultural oil treatment.

This is a good time for planting—though trees and shrubs planted in fall have more time to make roots in their new home before bud break occurs.

Fertilize established plants by side-dressing; follow label directions. Inspect for aphids and treat as described in Chapter Four.

Woody plants that bloom on the current year's growth typically need pruning early. Wait to prune those that bloom in spring or early summer on growth produced the previous year.

Bring in branches of spring-flowering shrubs and trees to enjoy.

SUMMER:

This is also an ideal time for planting container shrubs and trees, but they will need lots of water if the weather turns hot and dry.

Around the 4th of July it is usually appropriate to make a light application of fertilizer, 5-10-5 for flowering types, 14-14-14 timed release or 30-10-10 for foliage and all kinds needing acid soil.

Water deeply in times of drought.

Bring in branches of summer-flowering shrubs and trees to enjoy.

FALL:

An ideal season for setting out most container plants: the ground is warm, less likely to be waterlogged than in spring, and air temperatures are gradually decreasing, so the transplant directs energy toward establishing roots rather than making new top growth. If any newly planted trees or shrubs are in a windswept location, be sure to stake securely. Wrap trunks with burlap, or set up burlap screens to shield broadleaf evergreens from harsh northeast winds and direct sun early in the day.

Mulch with organic matter (leaf litter, pine straw, shredded bark and twigs, peat moss, and wood chips) at the base of trees and shrubs at this time.

Late fall through early winter is the time to enjoy evergreens and berried branches indoors.

WINTER:

Begin designing your border, hedge, or allée.

Early in the season is the time to side-dress around shrubs with several inches of well-rotted compost or cow manure. By spring this will have broken down into the surface soil, so that plenty of nutrients will be available to the plants and conditions will be conducive to growing.

Immediately after heavy snows, inspect the garden; use a broom to knock off any branch-threatening accumulations. In late winter through spring, bring in flowering branches of shrubs and trees.

In late winter through early spring, prune sparingly.

Chapter Two
The 100 Best Trees, Shrubs, and Ground Covers

ABELIA
(ab-BEE-lee-ah)

Abelia

CAPRIFOLIACEAE; honeysuckle family

Height/habit: Upright to cascading, 3–8 ft. (1–2.4 m.) high/wide, mostly in a range of 3–5 ft. (1–1.5 m.).

Leaves: Dimpled, oval, .5–1 in. (1.25–2.5 cm.) long; bronzy red at first, changing to glossy green in glossy abelia (*A.* x *grandiflora*); variously evergreen, deciduous, or semievergreen .

Flowers: Bell-like or tubular, to 1.5 in. (3.7 cm.) long, clustered at the axils and tips; white to pinkish white, lavender pink; *A. chinensis* fragrant. *A.* x *grandiflora* 'Edward Goucher' flowers profusely with purplish pink blooms.

Season: Summer into fall; after the flowers drop, coppery or reddish sepals remain indefinitely.

When to plant: Set transplants when available. Cold- and heat-tolerant zones 6–8 to 9–10.

Light: Sunny to partly shady.

Soil: Humusy, well drained, moist.

Fertilizer: 5-10-5 or 14-14-14 timed-release.

Pruning: Winter through spring, cut some of the oldest stems to the ground; shearing not recommended.

Propagation: Take cuttings in summer.

Uses: Specimen, borders, hedge, ground cover, cutting.

ACER
(A-sir)

Japanese Maple

ACERACEAE; maple family

Height/habit: *A. palmatum* small, gracefully branched tree, to 20 ft. (6 m.) high/wide.

Leaves: Palmately lobed into 5–11 parts, some lacily cut, 2–4 in. (5–10 cm.) long; all greens to purplish, bronze, or red.

Flowers: Inconspicuous.

Season: Foliage outstanding spring through fall.

When to plant: Set transplants when available. Cold- and heat-tolerant zones 5–9.

Light: Sunny (cooler climates) to partly shady (warmer).

Soil: Humusy, well drained, moist.

Fertilizer: 5-10-5 in spring, again early to midsummer. Soil too alkaline or salty causes brown leaf tips.

Pruning: In summer, emphasize tree's natural planed surfaces or encourage weeping form if at water's edge; cut frost-damaged wood 4 in. (10 cm.) into healthy wood.

Propagation: Take green-wood cuttings in summer, hardwood cuttings fall through winter.

Uses: Decorative understory tree for accent, especially in Japanese garden; containers; bonsai.

AESCULUS
(ESK-kew-luss)

Horse Chestnut; Scarlet Buckeye; Yellow Buckeye

HIPPOCASTANACEAE; buckeye family

Height/habit: Mound-forming shrubs and small trees 12–20 ft. (3.6–6 m.) high/wide, in the case of dwarf horse chestnut and the scarlet or yellow buckeyes (*A. parviflora* and *A. pavia*, respectively), to major shade trees, 75–100 ft. (22.7–30 m.) high/wide, as with red horse chestnut and standard horse chestnut (*A. x carnea* and *A. hippocastanum*, respectively).
Leaves: Compound, palmlike, 6–10 in. (15–25 cm.) across.
Flowers: Small, in showy panicles, to 8 in. (20 cm.) long; pink to dark red, greenish yellow, white, or yellow; white and fragrant in California buckeye (*A. californica*).
Season: Flowers spring through summer, followed by interesting fruit and winter branches.
When to plant: Set transplants when available. Cold- and heat-tolerant zones 3–5 to 9.
Light: Sunny to partly sunny.
Soil: Well drained, moist to on the dry side, slightly acidic.
Fertilizer: 5-10-5.
Pruning: Cut dead or broken branches any time; in general, prune before or after bloom.
Propagation: Sow newly harvested, ripe seeds in fall; layer or propagate from buds in spring.
Uses: Shade or understory trees; also for flowers and interesting fruit.

ARDISIA
(ar-DEE-zee-ah)

Coralberry; Spiceberry; Marlberry

MYRSINACEAE; myrsine family

Height/habit: Upright evergreen shrub, to 4 ft. (1.2 m.) high/wide in coralberry, sometimes also called spiceberry (*A. crenata*); evergreen ground cover shrub, 6–18 in. (15–45 cm.) high/wide in marlberry (*A. japonica*).
Leaves: Elliptic, crenate in coralberry, 3–4 in. (7.5–10 cm.) long; marlberry available in several forms having variegated leaves.

Flowers: Small, .25 in. (.63 cm.) across, in terminal or axillary cymes; white to pinkish; followed by berries that turn shiny, bright red and last well into the next flowering period.
Season: Spring for spiceberry, fall for marlberry; berries winter through spring.
When to plant: Set transplants when available. Cold- and heat-tolerant zones 6 (marlberry) to 9 (both species).
Light: Half-sunny to half-shady.
Soil: Humusy, well drained, moist.
Fertilizer: 5-10-5.
Pruning: Remove dead growth late winter through spring.
Propagation: Sow seeds winter through spring; take cuttings of half-ripened wood summer through fall.
Uses: Borders, ground cover, container.

BERBERIS
(BURR-burr-iss)

Barberry

BERBERIDACEAE; barberry family

Height/habit: Deciduous or evergreen spiny shrubs, 1–8 ft. (30–240 cm.) high/wide. Among outstanding garden types are the evergreen species Magellan barberry (*B. buxifolia*), Chilean barberry (*B. darwinii*), wintergreen barberry (*B. julianae*), and hybrid barberry (*B.* x *stenophylla*). Deciduous species include chalk-leaf barberry (*B. dictyophylla*) and Japanese barberry (*B. thunbergii*). There is also a semievergreen barberry (*B.* x *mentorensis*).

Leaves: Simple, to 1 in. (2.5 cm.) long; various greens, reds, or yellows.

Flowers: Small, bell-like, in umbels; yellow, orange; fruit red, purple, bluish black, or salmon.

Season: Flowers in spring; fruit colorful fall through winter.

When to plant: Set transplants when available. Cold- and heat-tolerant zones 4–6 to 9.

Light: Sunny to partly sunny.

Soil: Well drained, moist; deciduous types more drought-tolerant.

Fertilizer: 5-10-5.

Pruning: Remove dead growth and control size and shape winter through spring.

Propagation: Sow seeds fall through winter; take softwood cuttings in summer.

Uses: Borders, hedge, bonsai.

BETULA
(BET-yew-lah)

Birch

BETULACEAE; birch family

Height/habit: Large deciduous trees, 65–95 ft. (19.7–2 .8 m.), often with showy bark. Among noteworthy types are the Chinese paper birch (*B. albosinensis*); river birch (*B. nigra*); monarch birch (*B. maximowicziana*); carol, canoe, or paper birch (*B. papyrifera*); and the European birch (*B. pendula*).

Leaves: Oval to triangular, to 4 in. (10 cm.) long/wide.

Flowers: Catkins, 1–4 in. (2.5–10 cm.) long, males forming in the fall, persisting to spring, at which time the females appear.

Season: Always attractive.

When to plant: Set container transplants when available; otherwise, in spring with a ball of soil about the main roots. Cold- and heat-tolerant zones 2–5 to 7–8; river birch, zone 9.

Light: Sunny.

Soil: Well drained, moist.

Fertilizer: 14-14-14 timed-release at planting time.

Pruning: Remove dead or storm-damaged wood, cutting to the basal collar, whenever necessary.

Propagation: Sow seeds fall through winter.

Uses: Specimen, set in the open so that form and bark can be appreciated; bonsai.

BUDDLEIA
(BUD-lee-ah)

Buddleia; Fountain Butterfly Bush; Summer Lilac

LOGANIACEAE; logania family

Height/habit: Deciduous or evergreen shrubs or small trees, mostly 6–15 ft. (1.8–4.5 m.) high/wide. Excellent choices include the deciduous species fountain butterfly bush (*B. alternifolia*) and summer lilac (*B. davidii*), the semievergreen ball-flowered buddleia (*B. globosa*), and the evergreen South African buddleia (*B. auriculata*).

Leaves: Lance-shaped, 4–12 in. (10–30 cm.) long.

Flowers: Small, less than .5 in. (1.25 cm.), in dense, spikelike clusters, to 1 ft. (30 cm.) long; most colors; fragrant; attractive to hummingbirds and butterflies.

Season: Spring on previous year's growth in fountain butterfly bush; summer through fall for South African buddleia, fountain butterfly bush; summer through fall for South African buddleia, summer lilac, and ball-flowered buddleia. Prompt deadheading prolongs bloom and tidies appearance.

When to plant: Set transplants when available. Cold- and heat-tolerant zones 6–7 to 9–10.

Light: Sunny to half-sunny.

Soil: Humusy, well drained, moist.

Fertilizer: 5-10-5 or 14-14-14 timed-release.

Pruning: Cut back hard in spring before bloom; prune fountain butterfly bush after spring bloom.

Propagation: Take cuttings spring through fall.

Uses: Beds; borders; cottage, butterfly, and hummingbird gardens; containers.

BUXUS
(BUCKS-us)

Box

BUXACEAE; box family

Height/habit: Evergreen shrubs; Japanese box (*B. microphylla*) grows 3–6 ft. (1–1.8 m.) high/wide; common box (*B. sempervirens*) reaches small tree size, 25 ft. (7.5 m.). Korean box (*B. microphylla* var. *koreana*), grows 1.5 ft. (45 cm.) high, spreading to 4–5 ft. (1.2–1.5 m.) wide.

Leaves: Obovate to elliptic or lance-shaped, to 1 in. (2.5 cm.) long.

Flowers: Axillary clusters; inconspicuous.

Season: Always attractive.

When to plant: Set transplants when available. Cold- and heat-tolerant zones 4–7 to 9; Korean box most cold-hardy.

Light: Sunny to partly shady.

Soil: Well drained, moist.

Fertilizer: 14-14-14 timed-release.

Pruning: Prune late spring, after new growth has formed; also clean out dead leaves and twigs. To rejuvenate old box, reduce in stages as older wood could resist forming new shoots.

Propagation: Take cuttings late summer.

Uses: Hedge, borders, containers, bonsai.

CALLICARPA
(kal-ick-AR-pah)

Beautyberry

VERBENACEAE; verbena family

Height/habit: Deciduous shrubs, 4–9 ft. (1.2–2 .7 m.) high/wide. Noteworthy are American beautyberry (*C. americana*) and the smaller beautyberry (*C. dichotoma*).
Leaves: Elliptic to oval, 3–9 in. (7.5–22.5 cm.) long x half as wide, arranged at distant intervals along the stems.
Flowers: Very small but numerous in 1.5-in. (3.7-cm.) clusters above the leaf axils; pale blue to pink; followed by purple, blue, or white fruit.
Season: Best berry color late summer through fall.

When to plant: Set transplants when available. Cold- and heat-tolerant zones 6–7 to 9.
Light: Sunny to partly shady.
Soil: Humusy, well drained, moist.
Fertilizer: 5-10-5.
Pruning: Remove any dead wood and shape in spring. New growth will bloom and fruit the same year.
Propagation: Sow seeds fall through winter; take cuttings or layer in summer.
Uses: Beds; borders; specimen; containers; underplanting in shaded areas, such as among pine trees.

CALLISTEMON
(kal-iss-TEEM-on)

Bottlebrush

MYRTACEAE; myrtle family

Height/habit: Evergreen shrubs or small trees, generally 6–8 ft. (1.8–2.4 m.) but capable of growing to 30 ft. (9 m.). Noteworthy are lemon bottlebrush (*C. citrinus*) and narrowleafed bottlebrush (*C. linearis*).
Leaves: Narrow and lanceolate, to 4 in. (10 cm.) long; bronze when young.
Flowers: Showy heads or spikes, 2–4 in. (5–10 cm.) long, the stamens protruding so as to resemble the filaments of a bottlebrush; scarlet red.
Season: Spring through fall.

When to plant: Set transplants when available. Cold- and heat-tolerant zones 8–10; all zones for dwarf varieties in containers.
Light: Sunny.
Soil: Well drained, moist to on the dry side.
Fertilizer: 14-14-14 timed-release.
Pruning: Clean out any dead growth in spring; cutting back hard every third year promotes vigorous blooming.
Propagation: Sow seeds in spring; take semiripe cuttings late summer.
Uses: Beds, borders, specimen, espalier, containers (dwarf varieties), butterfly garden.

CALYCANTHUS
(kal-ee-KANTH-us)

Chinese Spicebush; Carolina Allspice

CALYCANTHACEAE; calycanthus family

Height/habit: Deciduous shrubs 4–10 ft. (1.2–3 m.) high/wide; spicily aromatic leaves, flowers, and fruits.
Leaves: Elliptic to oval, 5–8 in. (12.5–20 cm.) long.
Flowers: Flat or like small water lilies, to 2 in. (5 cm.) across; Carolina allspice (*C. floridus*) reddish brown, fragrant; Chinese spicebush (*C. chinensis*) noted for creamy white flowers.

Season: Late spring through summer.
When to plant: Set transplants when available. Cold- and heat-tolerant zones 5–9.
Light: Sunny (cooler climates) to half-shaded (warmer climates).
Soil: Humusy, well drained, moist.
Fertilizer: 5-10-5 or 14-14-14.
Pruning: Remove dead growth and generally thin shrub (favoring young wood) late winter through early spring.
Propagation: Sow seeds. Take cuttings, layer, or remove suckers spring through summer.
Uses: Beds, borders, specimen, containers.

CAMELLIA

(kah-MEE-lee-ah)

Camellia

THEACEAE; tea family

Height/habit: Evergreen shrubs to small trees, slow-growing, ultimately reaching 8–15 ft. (2.4–4.5 m.) high/wide. Especially outstanding are common camellia (*C. japonica*), compact Chinese camellia (*C. saluenensis*), netted camellia (*C. reticulata*), and sasanqua camellia (*C. sasanqua*).

Leaves: Oval to elliptic, 2–5 in. (5–12.5 cm.) long.

Flowers: Single, double, formal, and informal, 1–4 in. (2.5–10 cm.) across; most colors except blue; sasanqua camellia notably fragrant, as well as *C. rusticana* x *C. lutchuensis* 'Fragrant Pink,' *C. reticulata* 'Kramer's Supreme,' and *C. sasanqua* 'Chansonette.'

Season: Fall to spring; for longest season, select varieties indicated as early-, midseason-, and late-flowering.

When to plant: Set transplants when available. Heat- and cold-tolerant zones 7–8 to 9–10. Suited to containers all zones.

Light: Partly sunny (cooler climates) to partly shady (most gardens).

Soil: Humusy, well drained, moist.

Fertilizer: 5-10-10 labeled for use on camellias; side-dressing with cottonseed meal is an organic treatment.

Pruning: Clip to maintain shape and clean out all dead leaves and twiggy growths in spring after blooming.

Propagation: Sow seeds, take cuttings, or layer in spring.

Uses: Beds, borders, specimen, bonsai.

CARYOPTERIS
(karry-OPP-ter-iss)

Bluebeard

VERBENACEAE; verbena family

Height/habit: Rounded decidu-ous shrubs, 3–5 ft. (1–1.5 m.) high/wide. Especially notewor-thy is *Caryopteris* x *clandonensis*.

Leaves: Lance-shaped with toothed margins, 3–5 in. (7.5–12.5 cm.) long; leaf reverses silvery gray.

Flowers: Tiny, to .3 in. (.9 cm.) long, in showy clusters; blue.

Season: Late summer through fall.

When to plant: Set transplants when available. Cold- and heat-tolerant zones 5 (with protec-tion) to 9.

Light: Sunny to half-sunny.

Soil: Humusy, well drained, moist.

Fertilizer: 5-10-5 or 14-14-14.

Pruning: Cut back to green wood in spring; blooms appear on the same season's growth.

Propagation: Take cuttings summer through fall; sow seeds in spring.

Uses: Borders, containers, cottage and butterfly gardens.

CEANOTHUS
(see-ah-NO-thus)

California Lilac

RHAMNACEAE; buckthorn family

Height/habit: *C. thrysiflorus* evergreen shrub or tree, 2 ft. (61 cm.) high/wide in dwarf forms, up to 20–30 ft. (6–9 m.) high/wide.

Leaves: Oblong, to 2 in. (5 cm.) long.

Flowers: Small, growing in showy clusters at the branch tips; blue.

Season: Spring.

When to plant: Set transplants when available. Cold- and heat-tolerant zone 8; can be containerized in cooler zones and brought to a protected place in freezing weather.
Light: Sunny to half-sunny.
Soil: Well drained, moist to on the dry side.
Fertilizer: 5-10-5 or 14-14-14.
Pruning: After flowering, prune to within 4 in. (10 cm.) of the base of flowered growths.
Propagation: Take cuttings in summer; sow seeds in winter.
Uses: Wall shrub, espalier, specimen.

CEPHALANTHUS
(seff-al-ANTH-us)

Buttonbush

RUBIACEAE; madder family

Height/habit: *C. occidentalis* a deciduous shrub, 5–15 ft. (1.5–4.5 m.) high/wide.
Leaves: Glossy, oval-, elliptic-, or lance-shaped, to 6 in. (15 cm.) long.
Flowers: Small, to 1 in. (2.5 cm.) across, growing in showy globes; greenish white; fragrant.
Season: Summer.

When to plant: Set transplants when available. Cold- and heat-tolerant zones 4–9.
Light: Sunny to partly shady.
Soil: Well drained, moist to swampy.
Fertilizer: 5-10-5 or 14-14-14.
Pruning: Prune in early spring to maintain shape.
Propagation: Sow seeds or take mature wood cuttings in fall; take green-wood cuttings in spring.
Uses: Beds, borders, specimen.

CERCIS
(SUR-sis)

Eastern Redbud; Judas Tree; Raceme Redbud

LEGUMINOSAE; pea family

Height/habit: Deciduous shrubs or small trees, 15–40 ft. (4.5–12.1 m.) high by two-thirds as wide; frequently multi-trunked. Noteworthy are Eastern redbud (*C. canadensis*), Judas tree (*C. siliquastrum*), Chinese Judas tree (*C. chinensis*), and raceme redbud (*C. racemosa*).

Leaves: Kidney- or heart-shaped, with 2 upper lobes forming above both sides of the leaf stem, to 5 in. (12.5 cm.) wide; yellow fall color.

Flowers: Small, pealike, borne in dense clusters to 1 in. (2.5 cm.) across spaced around entire branch at regular intervals; white through pink, magenta, rose purple; followed by seed-pods resembling immature English pea pods.

Season: Early spring, before the new leaves. Old branches, to 20 years and more, have been known to flower, along with the main trunk.

When to plant: Set young transplants when available. Cold- and heat-tolerant zones 5–6 to 9–10.

Light: Sunny to partly shady.

Soil: Sandy, well drained, moist.

Fertillzer: 5-10-5 or 14-14-14.

Pruning: Cut only to shape or remove dead wood.

Propagation: Sow seeds, take cuttings, or layer summer through fall.

Uses: Borders, wild and shade gardens, understory tree, specimen, cutting to enjoy fresh or dried, bonsai.

CHAENOMELES
(kee-NOM-el-eez)

Japanese Flowering Quince

ROSACEAE; rose family

Height/habit: *C. speciosa* a deciduous, mostly spiny, shrub, 3–4 ft. (1–1.2 m.) to 10 ft. (3 m.) high/wide.

Leaves: Ovate to oblong, 1–4 in. (2.5–10 cm.) long.

Flowers: Resemble those of the apple, 1–2 in. (2.5–5 cm.) wide, single or double; scarlet, pink, white, apricot, coral, and most reds.

Season: Early spring, mostly before the new leaves.

When to plant: Set transplants when available. Cold- and heat-tolerant zones 5–9.

Light: Sunny.

Soil: Well drained, moist, not too alkaline.

Fertilizer: 14-14-14 timed-release.

Pruning: Any branches in need of pruning and not removed for forcing or fresh flowers can be cut after bloom time; cut side growths back to 2 or 3 buds; aim toward a bush that is fairly open through the center in order to show off the blooms.

Propagation: Sow seeds, take cuttings, layer, or graft summer through fall.

Uses: Beds, borders, cottage gardens, fan-shaped espalier, containers, bonsai, cutting (branches force well for winter bloom).

CHIONANTHUS
(kee-oh-NANTH-us)

Fringetree

OLEACEAE; olive family

Height/habit: Deciduous, multi
trunked, large shrubs or small
trees, easily 10–25 ft. (3–7.5 m.)
high/wide.

Leaves: Ovate to elliptic, to 4
in. (10 cm.) long; showy yellow
fall color.

Flowers: Fringelike, 4-petaled,
in clusters to 6 in. (15 cm.) long;
white followed by inedible blue
fruits, in grapelike clusters.

Season: Spring.

When to plant: Set transplants
when available. Cold- and
heat-tolerant zones 5–8 for
Chinese fringetree (*C. retusa*),
3–9 for common fringetree
(*C. virginicus*).

Light: Sunny.

Soil: Humusy, well drained,
moist.

Fertilizer: 14-14-14 timed-
release at planting; 5-10-5 as
general boost at beginning of
growing season.

Pruning: Remove dead wood in
spring.

Propagation: Sow seeds in
spring; take semiripe shoots in
early summer.

Uses: Background, specimen,
hedgerow.

CODIAEUM
(koh-DEE-um)

Croton
EUPHORBIACEAE; spurge family

Height/habit: *C. variegatum* var. *pictum* a bold tropical shrub, 6–12 ft. (1.8–3.6 m.) high/wide; grows to height of small tree in warmest climes.

Leaves: Linear to oval-lanceolate with smooth or undulating margins, leathery, 6–12 in. (15–30 cm.) long; all greens, reddish or cordovan, creamy to golden yellow, orange, rose pink, or apricot.

Flowers: Unusual, drooping racemes, to 8 in. (20 cm.) long; white.

Season: Best growth occurs in warm weather.

When to plant: Set transplants when available. Suited to planting in the ground zones 10–12; elsewhere container specimens can be placed outdoors in frost-free temperatures.

Light: Sunny to half-sunny.

Soil: Humusy, well drained, moist.

Fertilizer: 14-14-14 timed-release.

Pruning: Prune only to remove dead wood, usually spring at the beginning of active growth.

Propagation: Air-layer the most colorful branches spring through summer; take cuttings in high humidity and with bottom heat (in greenhouse, with soil-heating cables, or with electric blankets/sheets placed under pots and flats) winter through spring.

Uses: Colorful foliage accents for beds, borders, or background; specimen; container; cutting.

CORNUS
(KORN-us)

Dogwood;
Bunchberry;
Cornelian Cherry

CORNACEAE; dogwood family

Height/habit: Deciduous ground covers, multistemmed shrubs, and small trees, for example: bunchberry (*C. canadensis*) to 9 in. (22.5 cm.) high, spreading by woody rhizomes; red-osier dogwood (*C. sericea*) to 10 ft. (3 m.) high, forming colonies to 10–12 ft. (3.6 m.) wide; and Chinese dogwood (*C. kousa* var. *chinensis*) to 30 ft. (9 m.) high/wide.

Leaves: Oval to elliptic, 1–6 in. (2.5–15 cm.) long; excellent fall color.

Flowers: Small, but set off by showy, colorful bracts to 3 in. (7.5 cm.) across, before or after the leaves; white, pink, rose, red, or yellow.

Season: Spring through early summer.

When to plant: Set transplants when available; if root disturbance is involved, best early spring or late fall. Cold- and heat-tolerant zones 4-9, red-osier to zone 2, evergreen yellow-flowered dogwood (*C. capitata*) only zones 9–10.

Light: Sunny to half-shady.

Soil: Humusy, well drained, moist, acidic.

Fertilizer: 14-14-14 timed-release.

Pruning: Trees and ground covers need little cutting. Shrubby cornus, such as red-osier, grown for winter bark color need cutting back sharply in spring to induce growth for next cold season.

Propagation: Sow seeds, take cuttings, layer, or graft summer through fall.

Uses: Ground cover, borders, specimen, stream or pond banks, bonsai, cutting.

CORYLOPSIS
(korry-LOP-sis)

Winter Hazel

HAMAMELIDACEAE; witch-hazel family

Height/habit: Deciduous shrubs, 6–8 ft. (1.8–2.4 m.) high/wide. *C. pauciflora* and *C. spicata*, both called witch hazel, particularly noteworthy.
Leaves: Roundish, 2–4 in. (5–10 cm.) long; tinged pink at first, then bright green.
Flowers: Short, nodding clusters or drooping spikes, to 2 in. (5 cm.) long; yellow; fragrant.
Season: Early spring, before forsythia.

When to plant: Set transplants when available. Cold- and heat tolerant zones 6–8.
Light: Sunny to half-sunny.
Soil: Humusy, well drained, moist.
Fertilizer: 14-14-14 timed-release at planting; 5-10-5 as spring side-dressing.
Pruning: Little needed.
Propagation: Sow seeds or take cuttings summer through fall.
Uses: Beds, borders, cottage gardens, specimen, containers, bonsai, cutting.

COTINUS
(koh-TEE-nus)

Smoketree

ANACARDIACEAE; cashew family

Height/habit: *C. coggygria* a
deciduous shrub or small tree,
to 15 ft. (4.5 m.) high/wide.
Leaves: Elliptic, to 3 in. (7.5
cm.) long; blue-green in summer, yellow-orange-red in fall;
'Rubrifolia' has dark purple
foliage.
Flowers: Much-branched panicles, to 8 in. (20 cm.) long,
hairy pedicels; purplish,
"smoky."
Season: Early to midsummer.
When to plant: Set transplants
when available. Cold- and heat-
tolerant zones 5–6 to 8.
Light: Sunny.
Soil: Well drained, moist.
Fertilizer: 14-14-14 timed-
release.
Pruning: Little needed by
smoketree; purple-leaved forms
may be pruned back hard in
early spring to induce strong
shoots with large leaves.
Propagation: Sow seeds, layer,
or take root cuttings (for faith-
ful replicas of desirable fruiting
plants) in spring.
Uses: Border, specimen, wild or
prairie gardens, bonsai.

COTONEASTER
(koh-toh-nee-AST-er)

Cotoneaster; Rock Spray

ROSACEAE; rose family

Height/habit: Variously evergreen, as with Dammer evergreen (*C. dammeri*), semievergreen, as with box-leaved cotoneaster (*C. buxifolius*), or deciduous shrub, such as pointy-leaved cotoneaster (*C. apiculatus*), from ground covers like rock spray (*C. horizontalis*) that reach 1 ft. (30 cm.) high and twice as wide after several years, to high, arching branches reaching 20 ft. (6 m.), including *C. rehderi*. Other noteworthy species include creeping cotoneaster (*C. adpressa*), spreading cotoneaster (*C. divaricata*), small-leaved cotoneaster (*C. microphylla*), and willow-leaved cotoneaster (*C. salicifolia*).

Leaves: Round to elliptic, .5–1 in. (1.25–2.5 cm.) long.

Flowers: Small (to .25 in. [.63 cm.]), borne singly or in clusters, some showy; white, pink, reddish; berries bright red.

Season: Spring flowers, fall through winter fruit, all-year branch structure.

When to plant: Set transplants when available. Cold- and heat-tolerant zones 4–6 to 9, although not well adapted to hot, humid zones.

Light: Sunny to half-shady for high-pruned trees.

Soil: Well drained, moist to slightly dry.

Fertilizer: 14-14-14 timed-release.

Pruning: Remove dead parts in spring. Low-growers are ill suited to placement next to walks since cutting them back results in unattractive stubs.

Propagation: Take cuttings or layer spring through summer; sow seeds in fall.

Uses: Ground cover, rock gardens, specimen, container, bonsai, cutting.

CRATAEGUS
(krah-TEE-jus)

Hawthorn

ROSACEAE; rose family

Height/habit: Deciduous, spiny shrubs or small trees, 20–30 ft. (6–9 m.) high/wide. Especially good performers are Arnold hawthorn (*C. arnoldiana*), Kansas hawthorn (*C. cocciniodes*), cockspur thorn (*C. crusgallii*), hybrid hawthorn (*C. x lavalleii*), Eastern hawthorn (*C. mollis*), May haw (*C. opaca*), English hawthorn (*C. oxyacantha*), Washington hawthorn (*C. phaenopyrum*), and green haw (*C. viridis*).
Leaves: Often lobed, 2–4 in.

(5–10 cm.) long; brilliant fall color in some, ranging from yellow to scarlet, red, orange, and bronze shades.
Flowers: Similar to apple blossoms, single or double, in showy clusters, to 2 in. (5 cm.) across; white, pink, cerise, carmine, crimson, or purple; fruit ornamental as well as edible, *C. opaca* 'Louisiana Choice' notably good for making jelly.
Season: Flowers late spring through early summer, fruit and foliage color in fall.
When to plant: Set transplants when available. Cold- and heat-tolerant zones 4–6 to 9; it is important to purchase a

crataegus known to be locally adapted.
Light: Sunny.
Soil: Well drained, moist.
Fertilizer: 14-14-14 timed-release at planting time, 5-10-5 thereafter.
Pruning: Train trees and remove dead wood early spring through summer.
Propagation: Layer in summer; sow seeds fall through winter. Seedlings of natives can sometimes be transplanted in spring.
Uses: Hedges, ornamental trees, windbreaks and hedgerows, espalier, bonsai, cutting.

CYDONIA
(sigh-DOH-nee-ah)

Quince

ROSACEAE; rose family

Height/habit: Common quince
(*C. oblonga*) a small deciduous
tree, to 20 ft. (6 m.) high by
two-thirds as wide.
Leaves: Oval to oblong, to 4 in.
(10 cm.) long.
Flowers: Similar to apple blossoms, to 2 in. (5 cm.) across;
white to pink; fruit apple- or
pear-shaped, 3–4 in. (7.5–10
cm.) in diameter, bright yellow.
Season: Flowers spring, fruit
late summer through fall.
When to plant: Set transplants
when available, allowing 20 ft.
(6 m.) between trees. Cold-
and heat-tolerant zones 4–8;
C. sinensis to zone 9.
Light: Sunny.
Soil: Well drained, moist.
Fertilizer: 5-10-5.
Pruning: Remove surplus
branches late winter through
spring; little needed.
Propagation: Take hardwood
cuttings fall through winter.
Uses: Shade, specimen, fruit,
bonsai.

CYTISUS
(SIT-ih-sus)

Broom

LEGUMINOSAE; pea family

Height/habit: Deciduous or persistent-leaved shrubs, upright or fountainlike, 1–10 ft. (30–300 cm. [3 m.]) high/wide. Spike broom (*C. nigricans*), purple broom (*C. purpureus*), and Scotch broom (*C. scoparius*) especially good performers.

Leaves: Simple or trifoliate, .5–.75 in. (1.25–2 cm.) long.

Flowers: Pealike, to 1 in. (2.5 cm.) across, growing in dense clusters or scattered along the stems; white, yellow, orange, red, or purplish; often fragrant.

Season: Spring through summer.

When to plant: Set transplants when available; disturb roots as little as possible. Cold- and heat-tolerant zones 5–7 to 8–9.

Light: Sunny.

Soil: Well drained, moist to on the dry side; locally adapted species drought-tolerant when established.

Fertilizer: 5-10-5. Yellowish leaves could indicate soil too alkaline; apply chelated iron or 30-10-10.

Pruning: Immediately after flowering, cut back new wood by two-thirds; cutting into old wood not advised as it rarely breaks into vigorous new growth.

Propagation: Sow newly ripened seeds summer through fall; take 2–4-in.- (5–10 cm.-) long cuttings in summer.

Uses: Specimen, borders, cottage or rock gardens, cutting.

DAPHNE
(DAFF-nee)

Daphne; Garland Flower

THYMELACEAE; mezereum family

Height/habit: Small deciduous and evergreen shrubs, 1–4 ft. (1.2 m.) high/wide. Deciduous garden favorites include Caucasus daphne (*D. caucasica*), lilac daphne (*D. genkwa*), and February daphne (*D. mezereum*). Evergreen choices include garland flower (*D. cneorum*) and winter daphne (*D. odora*).

Leaves: Oblong to lance-shaped, 2–3 in. (5–7.5 cm.) long.

Flowers: Small, .5 in. (1.25 cm.) across, in dense terminal heads; white, rose pink, lilac, purple, or pink; fragrant.

Season: Late winter through spring.

When to plant: Set transplants when available. Cold- and heat-tolerant zones 4–8.

Light: Sunny to partly sunny.

Soil: Humusy, well drained, moist; slightly acidic.

Fertilizer: 14-14-14 timed-release.

Pruning: Cut only to shape or to remove dead wood after flowering.

Propagation: Sow seeds fall through winter; take cuttings or layer in spring.

Uses: Beds, borders, specimen, container, espalier, cottage and rock gardens, bonsai, cutting.

DELONIX
(dee-LON-ix)

Royal Poinciana

LEGUMINOSAE; pea family

Height/habit: *D. regia* a wide-branching tree, to 40 ft. (12.1 m.) high/wide or more.
Leaves: Fernlike, pinnate, growing to 2 ft. (61 cm.) long.
Flowers: To 4 in. (10 cm.) wide, appearing in clusters; bright scarlet or yellow.
Season: Summer.

When to plant: Set transplants when available. Limited to frost-free gardens, zone 10; could live some years if in protected site zone 9.
Light: Sunny.
Soil: Well drained, moist.
Fertilizer: 5-10-5.
Pruning: Shape in winter; remove weak or dead wood after flowering.
Propagation: Sow seeds spring through summer.
Uses: Specimen, lawn, shade.

DEUTZIA
(DEWT-zee-ah)

Deutzia

SAXIFRAGACEAE; saxifrage family

Height/habit: Low to medium, spreading, mostly deciduous shrubs, 3–8 ft. (1–2.4 m.) high/wide. Best choices are semidwarf deutzia (*D. crenata*), *D.* x *elegantissima* 'Rosealind,' slender or spreading deutzia (*D. gracilis*), *D.* x *hybrida* 'Contraste,' *D. scabra* 'Pride of Rochester,' and early deutzia (*D.* x *rosea* 'Grandiflora'). *D. crenata* 'Nakata' is a ground cover.

Leaves: Slender, curving, oblong- to lance-shaped, 2–3 in. (5–7.5 cm.) long, slightly hairy.

Flowers: Tubular, 5-lobed, to 1 in. (2.5 cm.) across, growing in clusters; white, pink, or rose pink.

Season: Late spring to early summer.

When to plant: Set transplants when available. Cold- and heat-tolerant zones 4–5 to 8; semidwarf deutzia zones 6–9.

Light: Sunny to half-sunny.

Soil: Well drained, moist.

Fertilizer: 5-10-5.

Pruning: As soon as the flowers fade, cut back to strong new shoots. Periodically remove 1 or 2 stems to the ground to simulate young shoots.

Propagation: Sow newly ripened seeds, take cuttings, or layer summer through fall.

Uses: Beds, borders, specimen, ground cover, bonsai.

ELAEAGNUS
(el-ee-AG-nus)

Russian Olive; Silverberry; Gumi

ELAEAGNACEAE; oleaster family

Height/habit: Shrubs or small trees, deciduous or evergreen, 6–20 ft. (1.8–6 m.) high/wide. Among deciduous choices are Russian olive (*E. angustifolia*), silverberry (*E. commutata*), Gumi (*E. multiflora*), and silver elaeagnus (*E. umbellata*). Thorny elaeagnus (*E. pungens*) is evergreen.

Leaves: Elliptic, 3–4 in. (7.5–10 cm.) long, covered with silver to brown scales, resulting in a silver-and-gold effect; variegated creamy to yellow in some cultivars.

Flowers: Inconspicuous, .5–1 in. (1.25–2.5 cm.), borne on stems below the leaves; white or yellow; very fragrant; followed by yellow, pink, or red fruit.

Season: Flowers in spring; fruit, summer through fall; plants attractive in all seasons.

When to plant: Set transplants when available. Cold- and heat-tolerant zones 3–4 to 9, with the exception of thorny elaeagnus, zones 6–10.

Light: Sunny to shady.

Soil: Humusy, well drained, moist.

Fertilizer: 14-14-14 timed-release.

Pruning: Deciduous types can be cut back hard in early spring; cut thorny elaeagnus as necessary from spring through early summer or fall through winter, using the cut branches for flower arrangements; promptly remove any plain green shoots appearing on a variegated plant.

Propagation: Sow seeds or take hardwood cuttings fall through winter; layer spring through summer.

Uses: Borders, specimen, espalier, containers, hedge, seaside gardens, bonsai, cutting.

ENKIANTHUS
(enk-ee-ANTH-us)

Bellflower Enkianthus

ERICACEAE; heath family

Height/habit: *E. campanulatus* a deciduous shrub, 15–30 ft. (1.5–9 m.) high/wide.

Leaves: Elliptic to ovate, to 3 in. (7.5 cm.) long, in whorls at the branch tips; brilliant scarlet fall color.

Flowers: Bell-like, resembling lily of the valley, to .5 in. (1.25 cm.) long, in drooping clusters; white to pale yellowish to orange and red with dark red veins; followed by smooth orange-yellow fruit.

Season: Late spring to early summer.

When to plant: Set transplants when available. Cold- and heat-tolerant zones 5–7.

Light: Half-sunny to half-shady.

Soil: Humusy, well drained, moist, acidic.

Fertilizer: 14-14-14 timed-release.

Pruning: Only cut to size and shape immediately after flowering.

Propagation: Sow seeds, take cuttings, or layer summer through fall.

Uses: Borders, specimen, espalier, bonsai.

ERYTHRINA
(airy-THREYE-nah)

Coral Tree; Coral Bean; Cardinal Spear

LEGUMINOSAE; pea family

Height/habit: Thorny sub-shrubs 6–12 ft. (1.8–3.6 m.) high/wide, to full-grown trees 40–60 ft. (12.1–18.2 m) high/wide. Excellent showy choices are hybrid coral tree (*E.* x *bidwillii*); cockspur coral tree (*E. crista-galli*); *E. flabelli-formis*; and coral bean, also known as cardinal spear (*E. herbacea*).

Leaves: Composed of 3 leaflets united to a single stem, to 3 in. (7.5 cm.) long or more.
Flowers: Similar to those of butterfly pea, spreading or fold-ing, 1–5 in. (2.5–12.5 cm.) across, growing in erect racemes to 2 ft. (61 cm.); red, orange, pink, or rose.
Season: Late spring through summer.
When to plant: Set transplants when available. Cold- and heat-tolerant zones 7–8 to 10. Herbaceous types treated as root-hardy perennials at the colder limits, more shrublike in the tropics.

Light: Sunny.
Soil: Well drained, moist to on the dry side; becomes drought-tolerant with age.
Fertilizer: 5-10-5.
Pruning: Cut back to healthy green wood or all the way to the ground, as appropriate, in spring. Flowers appear on new growth.
Propagation: Sow seeds spring through summer; take woody cuttings summer through fall.
Uses: Hedgerow, borders, accent.

EUONYMUS
(yew-ON-ee-mus)

Dwarf Burning Bush; Strawberry Bush; Cork Bush; Wintercreeper; Evergreen Euonymus

CELASTRACEAE; staff-tree family

Height/habit: Deciduous or evergreen shrubs and small trees, 1.5 ft. (45 cm.) to 20 ft. (6 m.) high/wide. Fine deciduous choices are dwarf burning bush (*E. alata* 'Compacta') and strawberry bush (*E. americana*). Wintercreeper (*E. fortunei*) and evergreen euonymus (*E. japonicus*) retain their leaves year-round.

Leaves: Ovate-, elliptic- or lance-shaped, 1–3 in. (2.5–7.5 cm.) long; some evergreens notably variegated silvery to bright golden yellow; fall color outstanding in dwarf burning bush. Bare winter branches noteworthy in cork bush, also known as winged euonymus (*E. alata*).

Flowers: Small, inconspicuous, in axillary cymes; green, purple; showy fruits may be pink, orange, or red.

Season: Attractive all year.

When to plant: Set transplants when available. Cold- and heat-tolerant zones 3–5 to 9; *A. alata* and varieties zones 3–8.

Light: Sunny to half-sunny.

Soil: Humusy, well drained, moist; deciduous types can be drought- and wind-tolerant.

Fertilizer: 5-10-5.

Pruning: Prune deciduous types only to remove dead wood or in winter if they form clipped hedge; remove from variegated types any branches that revert to plain green leaves.

Propagation: Take cuttings summer through fall.

Uses: Borders, accent, hedge, ground cover, seaside gardens, espalier, bonsai, cutting.

EXOCHORDA
(ex-oh-KOR-dah)

The Bride

ROSACEAE; rose family

Height/habit: *E. macrantha* a deciduous, weeping shrub, to 4 ft. (1.2 m.) high/wide.
Leaves: Rounded, 1–2 in. (2.5–5 cm.) across.
Flowers: Showy, 1–2 in. (2.5–5 cm.) across, growing in loose clusters; white.
Season: Spring.
When to plant: Set transplants when available. Cold- and heat-tolerant zones 5–9.
Light: Sunny to half-sunny.
Soil: Well drained, moist to wet.
Fertilizer: 5-10-5.
Pruning: To rejuvenate old, neglected plants cut back hard in early spring.
Propagation: Sow newly ripened seeds or take cuttings summer through fall.
Uses: Borders, accent, cottage gardens.

FAGUS
(FAY-gus)

Beech

FAGACEAE; beech family

Height/habit: Stately deciduous trees, 80–100 ft. (24–30 m.) high/wide.

Leaves: Serrated—though less so in the European beech (*F. sylvatica*)—to ovate, to 4 in. (10 cm.) long; American beech (*F. grandifolia*) turns clear yellow in fall. Also worth growing is weeping beech (*F. sylvatica* 'Pendula').

Flowers: Males in drooping heads, inconspicuous.

Season: Attractive all year.

When to plant: Set transplants when available. Do not disturb taproot. Cold- and heat-tolerant zones 3–5 to 9.

Light: Sunny to half-sunny.

Soil: Humusy, well drained, moist, acidic.

Fertilizer: 14-14-14 timed-release.

Pruning: Cut only to remove dead or damaged wood.

Propagation: Sow seeds fall through winter. Containerize seedlings to prevent taproot from becoming deeply established in the ground.

Uses: Shade, windbreak, clipped hedge, bonsai.

FEIJOA
(fay-JOH-uh)
Pineapple Guava
MYRTACEAE; myrtle family

Height/habit: *F. sellowiana* an evergreen shrub or small tree, to 225 ft. (68 m.) high/wide.
Leaves: Elliptic to oblong, to 3 in. (7.5 cm.) long, green above, woolly beneath.
Flowers: Cup-shaped, to 1.5 in. (3.7 cm.) across, 4 petals fleshy, eaten in salads; white outside, purplish red inside, with dark red stamens; edible fruit 2–3 in. (5–7.5 cm.) long, green tinged red, tasting of guava.
Season: Flowers in spring; fruit follows in 4–7 months.

When to plant: Set transplants when available. Cold- and heat-tolerant zones 8–10.
Light: Sunny.
Soil: Humusy, well drained, moist.
Fertilizer: 5-10-5.
Pruning: Control and guide growth in spring.
Propagation: Sow seeds or take cuttings spring through summer; graft named varieties winter through spring.
Uses: Borders, specimen, hedge, espalier, edible fruit, containers.

FORSYTHIA
(for-SITH-ee-ah)
Forsythia
OLEACEAE; olive family

Height/habit: Deciduous shrubs of loosely spreading form, 1.5 ft. (45 cm.) to 10 ft. (3 m.) high/wide. Excellent choices are border forsythia (*F.* x *intermedia*), weeping forsythia (*F. suspensa*), and green-stem forsythia (*F. viridissima*).
Leaves: Often 3-lobed, to 6 in. (15 cm.) long.
Flowers: Precede the leaves, 1 in. (2.5 cm.) across, growing in clusters around the branches; every shade of yellow from pale to bright to dark.
Season: Early spring.

When to plant: Set transplants when available. Cold- and heat-tolerant zones 4–8, green-stem zones 5–9. Protracted cold below zero can kill flower buds.
Light: Sunny.
Soil: Well drained, moist.
Fertilizer: 5-10-5.
Pruning: To control growth, remove some branches for forcing in winter, others while coming into bloom; when flowering finishes, cut back to the ground some of the oldest branches.
Propagation: Take cuttings of green wood or ground-layer the tips spring through summer.
Uses: Borders, unclipped hedge, espalier, containers (dwarfs), bonsai, cutting.

FOTHERGILLA
(foth-uhr-GILL-ah)

Witch Alder

HAMAMELIDACEAE; witch-hazel
family

Height/habit: Deciduous,
spreading shrubs, 3–10 ft. (1–3
m.) high/wide. Of note are
Eastern dwarf witch alder
(*F. gardenii* 'Eastern Form')
and American witch alder
(*F. major*).

Leaves: Round to oval, 3–4 in.
(7.5–10 cm.) long; long-lasting
red color in fall.

Flowers: Precede the leaves;
feathery tufts or cylindrical
spikes, comprised of bundled
filaments or stamens; white.

Season: Blooms in spring,
foliage color in fall.

When to plant: Set transplants
when available. Cold- and heat-
tolerant zones 5–8.

Light: Sunny to partly sunny.

Soil: Humusy, well drained,
moist.

Fertilizer: 5-10-5.

Pruning: Little needed.

Propagation: Layer spring
through fall; it can take 2 years
to strike roots.

Uses: Borders, specimen.

FRANKLINIA
(frank-LIN-ee-ah)

Franklin Tree

THEACEAE; tea family

Height/habit: *F. alatamaha* a small, deciduous tree, 20–30 ft. (6–9 m.) high.
Leaves: Oblong, 4–6 in. (10–15 cm.) long, clustered at the tips of new growth; turning scarlet in fall.
Flowers: Open flat from round buds, 3–4 in. (7.5–10 cm.) across, with yellow stamens prominent in center; creamy white.
Season: Flowers late summer, often coinciding with changing leaf colors.

When to plant: Set transplants when available. Cold- and heat-tolerant zones 4–9.
Light: Sunny to partly shady.
Soil: Humusy, well drained, moist, acidic.
Fertilizer: 14-14-14 or 5-10-5.
Pruning: Little needed.
Propagation: Sow seeds spring through summer; they bloom in up to 7 years; take half-ripe cuttings summer through fall.
Uses: Specimen for garden, lawn, or patio; companion for azaleas and rhododendrons.

FUCHSIA
(FEW-shuh)

Fuchsia

ONAGRACEAE; evening-primrose family

Height/habit: Deciduous to evergreen shrubs (depending on climate and growing conditions), from tidy shrublets to upright bushes, tree-form standards, or hanging baskets, 1–15 ft. (30–450 cm. [4.5 m.]) high/wide. Well worth growing are common fuchsia (*F.* x *hybrida*), hummingbird fuchsia (*F. magellanica*), and honeysuckle fuchsia (*F. triphylla* 'Gartenmeister Bohnstedt').

Leaves: Oval, from .5 in. (1.25 cm.) to 6–7 in. (15–17 cm.) long.

Flowers: Hanging, solitary, or bunched, single or double, 1–4 in. (2.5–10 cm.) across; all colors except oranges and yellows, often strikingly bicolored.

Season: Spring through summer.

When to plant: Set transplants when available. Cold- and heat-hardy in a fairly narrow range, around zone 8, but grown elsewhere as tender perennials, wintered in a frost-free place.

Light: Sunny (cooler climates) to shady.

Soil: Humusy, well drained, moist; dry side acceptable in winter.

Fertilizer: 14-14-14 timed-release.

Pruning: Remove any dead wood in spring; for baskets, bushes, and tree-form standards, cut back by half to two-thirds at the beginning of the new season.

Propagation: Take cuttings spring through summer; sow seeds winter through spring.

Uses: Borders, containers, hanging garden, window boxes, espalier, bonsai.

GARDENIA
(gar-DEE-nee-ah)

Gardenia; Cape Jasmine

RUBIACEAE; madder family

Height/habit: Evergreen shrublets or shrubs, 1–10 ft. (30–300 cm. [3 m.]) high/wide.

Leaves: Leathery, lance-shaped to ovate, to 4 in. (10 cm.) long.

Flowers: Single extended tubes in single gardenia (*G. thunbergia*), doubled in common gardenia, also known as Cape jasmine (*G. jasminoides*), 2–3 in. (5–7.5 cm.) across; velvety white; fragrant.

Season: Spring through summer through fall, depending on variety and climate.

When to plant: Set transplants when available. Cold- and heat-tolerant zones 8–9 to 10; in colder zones place containers outdoors in warm weather.

Light: Sunny to half-sunny.

Soil: Humusy, well drained, moist, acidic.

Fertilizer: 30-10-10 or 14-14-14 timed-release.

Pruning: Little needed, only to remove dead branches or to thin out twiggy cross-branching from interior of the plant.

Propagation: Take cuttings spring through summer or in winter with bottom heat (in greenhouse, with soil-heating cables, or with electric blankets/sheets placed under pots and flats).

Uses: Borders, specimen, containers, tree-form standard, bonsai, cutting.

GINKGO
(GINK-go)

Ginkgo;
Maidenhair Tree

GINKGOACEAE; ginkgo family

Height/habit: *G. biloba* deciduous tree, to 120 ft. (36.4 m.) high.

Leaves: Distinctly fanned into 2 lobes, to 2 in. (5 cm.) across, reminiscent of maidenhair fern; turning rapidly golden in fall, then falling all at once into a glowing carpet.

Flowers: Male (staminate) and female (pistillate) on separate plants; female flowers in loose catkins followed by oval fruit, greenish golden when ripe and smelling of rancid butter, edible, considered a delicacy by some.

Season: Satisfactory at all times.

When to plant: Set transplants when available. Cold- and heat-tolerant zones 3–9. Unless the fruit is desired, male clones are recommended, such as 'Compacta,' 'Fairmount,' 'Fastigiata,' 'Lakeview,' 'Old Gold,' and 'Saratoga.'

Light: Sunny.

Soil: Well drained, moist.

Fertilizer: 14-14-14 timed-release.

Pruning: Little needed, except to shape or remove dead parts. Staking helps young trees.

Propagation: Take cuttings from males or sow seeds fall through winter.

Uses: Shade, street, lawn, specimen, bonsai.

HALESIA
(hay-LEE-zee-ah)

Silver Bell;
Snowdrop Tree

STYRACACEAE; storax family

Height/habit: Deciduous trees, 40–50 ft. (12.1–15 m.) high/wide.
Leaves: Oval to oblong, 4–8 in. (10–20 cm.) long.
Flowers: Pendulous, bell-shaped, .75–1 in. (2–2.5 cm.) long, set along the branches; white or, rarely, pink.
Season: Spring.
When to plant: Set transplants when available. Cold- and heat-tolerant zones 4–5 to 8–9.
Light: Sunny (cool climates) to partly shady/protected (hotter climates).

Soil: Humusy, well drained, moist.
Fertilizer: 14-14-14 timed-release.
Pruning: Immediately after flowering, oldest flowered shoots may be removed to encourage new ones and attractive form.
Propagation: Layer or take root cuttings spring through summer; sow seeds in fall.
Uses: Borders, background, woodland and cottage gardens, cutting.

HAMAMELIS
(ham-am-MEEL-iss)

Witch Hazel

HAMAMELIDACEAE; witch-hazel family

Height/habit: Deciduous shrubs or trees, 6–30 ft. (1.8–9 m.) high/wide. Hybrid witch hazel (*H.* x *intermedia*), Japanese witch hazel (*H. japonica*), Chinese witch hazel (*H. mollis*), Dwarf Ozark witch hazel (*H. vernalis*), and common witch hazel (*H. virginiana*) are all excellent choices.
Leaves: Roundish, 4–6 in. (10–15 cm.) long; fall color yellow or orange.
Flowers: Ribbonlike, to 1 in. (2.5 cm.) long, in dense clusters; yellow, orange, or red; fragrant.

Season: Late winter through earliest spring, with the exception of common witch hazel, which blooms in late fall.
When to plant: Set transplants when available. Cold- and heat-tolerant zones 4–5 to 8.
Light: Sunny to half-shady.
Soil: Humusy, well drained, moist.
Fertilizer: 14-14-14 timed-release at planting or 5-10-5.
Pruning: Little needed, except for long branches that extend beyond the general outline of the bush; do so at flowering time so as to enjoy the cut branches indoors.
Propagation: Layer in summer; sow seeds in fall.
Uses: Borders, cottage gardens, screening, specimen, espalier, bonsai.

HAMELIA
(ham-EE-lee-ah)

Fire Bush; Hummingbird Bush

RUBIACEAE; madder family

Height/habit: *H. patens*, called both fire bush and hummingbird bush, an evergreen shrub or small tree, to 25 ft. (7.5 m.).
Leaves: Elliptic to ovate, to 6 in. (15 cm.) long; green to golden in summer, glowing red in fall.
Flowers: Tubular, to 1 in. (2.5 cm.) long, growing in terminal clusters; reddish orange. Attractive to both butterflies and hummingbirds.
Season: Summer through fall; foliage color persists in mild-winter climates.

When to plant: Set transplants when available, usually spring through summer. Cold- and heat-tolerant zones 9–10.
Light: Sunny to half-sunny.
Soil: Humusy, well drained, moist.
Fertilizer: 14-14-14 timed-release, 5-10-5 or 15-30-15 at onset of bloom season.
Pruning: Cut back to green wood in late spring; even if killed to the ground, the root-stocks often survive and send up new shoots that bloom the same season.
Propagation: Take cuttings spring through summer.
Uses: Beds, borders, containers, hedge, butterfly and hummingbird gardens.

HEDERA
(HED-der-ah)

Ivy

ARALIACEAE; aralia family

Height/habit: Evergreen vines becoming shrublike with age, size (length) dictated by the site and method of training, as well as by the variety or cultivar.

Leaves: Distinctly lobed and pointed, .5–4 in. (1.25–10 cm.) long; various greens, also variegated gold, white, creamy, or silver.

Flowers: Inconspicuous; appear only on mature ivies, followed by berries.

Season: Attractive at most times.

When to plant: Set transplants when available. Cold- and heat-tolerant zones 8–10 for Algerian ivy (*H. canariensis*), 4–9 for smaller-leaved English ivy (*H. helix*).

Light: Sunny to shady.

Soil: Humusy, well drained, moist.

Fertilizer: 14-14-14 timed-release.

Pruning: Only to remove dead growth or to curtail any that is overextended.

Propagation: Set tip cuttings to root in clean, moist medium in bright light and moderate temperatures (50–70°F [10–21°C]).

Uses: Ground cover; wall climber; mature form as shrub specimen, espalier, and topiary; bonsai; cutting.

HIBISCUS
(high-BISK-us)

Texas Star; Swamp Mallow; Confederate Rose; Chinese Hibiscus; Rose of Sharon

MALVACEAE; mallow family

Height/habit: Upright herbaceous or woody shrubs to small trees, 3–15 ft. (1–4.5 m.) high/wide. Of note for the garden are Texas star (*H. coccineus*), swamp mallow (*H. moscheutos* 'Disco Belle,' 'Southern Belle'), Confederate rose (*H. mutabilis*), Chinese hibiscus (*H. rosa-sinensis*), fringe-petalled hibiscus (*H. schizopetalus)*, and rose of Sharon (*H. syriacus*).

Leaves: Palmate, ovate to elliptic, heart-shaped, or triangular with lobes, 1–6 in. (2.5–15 cm.); tropical species glossy or shiny.

Flowers: Cups or saucers, 2–10 in. (5–25 cm.) across, appearing at the branch tips on new wood; most colors.

Season: Spring through summer; Chinese hibiscus most of the year in frost-free climates.

When to plant: Set transplants when available. Cold- and heat-tolerant zones 5–9 for swamp mallow and rose of Sharon, 9–10 for the tropical species.

Light: Sunny.

Soil: Humusy, well drained, moist, acidic.

Fertilizer: 7-2-7 or 10-2-4 for Chinese hibiscus; 14-14-14 for general growth boost.

Pruning: Remove dead wood or prune to guide and train in spring—it may be necessary to cut it to the ground.

Propagation: Sow seeds, take cuttings, or layer spring through summer.

Uses: Beds, borders, specimen, screening, containers, cutting.

HYDRANGEA
(high-DRAIN-jee-uh)

Hydrangea
SAXIFRAGACEAE; saxifrage family

Height/habit: Mostly deciduous shrubs or climbers, 6 to 20 ft. (1.8–6 m.) high/wide or more. Climbing hydrangea (*H. anomala* var. *petiolaris*), hills-of-snow (*H. arborescens*), French hydrangea (*H. macrophylla*), peegee hydrangea (*H. paniculata* var. *grandiflora*), and Snow Queen oakleaf hydrangea (*H. quercifolia* 'Snow Queen') are excellent garden choices.

Leaves: Roundish to ovate or similar to oak leaf, 4–6 in. (10–15 cm.) long; some varieties variegated silvery white.

Flowers: Dense clusters, few or many showy; lacy fertile flowers surrounded by sterile; white, blue, pink, purplish mauve, or white turning pale green in peegee hydrangea.

Season: Spring through summer through fall, depending on the species and the local weather.

When to plant: Set transplants when available. Cold- and heat-tolerant zones 4–6 to 8–9.

Light: Sunny to partly shady.

Soil: Humusy, well drained, moist; acidic for blue flowers in the colored strains of French hydrangea.

Fertilizer: 14-14-14 timed-release; 30-10-10 for more acidity.

Pruning: Remove old shoots from French hydrangea after flowering. Hydrangeas that bloom on current season's growth can be cut back as sharply as needed in early spring.

Propagation: Take cuttings or layer summer through fall.

Uses: Beds, borders, specimen, hedge, wall or fence cover, containers, seaside and cottage gardens, cutting.

ILEX
(EYE-lex)

Holly; Winterberry; Yaupon
AQUIFOLIACEAE; holly family

Height/habit: Evergreen or deciduous shrubs or trees, 1–80 ft. (30–240 cm. [24 m.]) high/wide. Among evergreen favorites are English holly (*I. aquifolium*), Chinese holly (*I. cornuta*), Japanese holly (*I. crenata*), American holly (*I. opaca*), and yaupon (*I. vomitoria*). Winterberry (*I. verticillata*) is deciduous.

Leaves: Often tipped with spines 1.5–3 in. (3.7–7.5 cm.) long; various greens, often variegated creamy or yellow.

Flowers: Male (staminate) and female (pistillate) on different plants, inconspicuous; white or greenish; followed by berries in range of colors.

Season: Attractive all year.

When to plant: Set transplants when available. Cold- and heat-tolerant zones 3–7 to 9.

Light: Sunny.

Soil: Humusy, well drained, moist.

Fertilizer: 14-14-14 or 5-10-5.

Pruning: Trim lightly as growth begins in spring; also remove any dead branches or tips damaged by winter. To rejuvenate old hollies, cut back sharply in spring. Holly hedges need shearing midsummer. Cuttings removed for holiday decorations count also as pruning.

Propagation: Take cuttings of deciduous types in summer and hardwood cuttings of evergreen types fall through winter.

Uses: Beds, borders, screening, specimen, hedge, espalier, tree-form standard, bonsai, cutting.

INDIGOFERA
(in-dig-GOFF-er-ah)

Indigo

LEGUMINOSAE; pea family

Height/habit: Deciduous shrubs or perennial herbs 5–6 ft. (1.5–1.8 m.) high/wide. Popular choices are pink indigo (*I. amblyantha*), Asian indigo (*I. kirilowii*), and Chinese indigo (*I. potaninii*).

Leaves: Odd-numbered leaflets, often 5–7 or 9–11, to 6 in. (15 cm.) long.

Flowers: Gracefully drooping clusters, 5–7 in. (12.5–17 cm.) long; lilac pink, rose, lilac purple, or white.

Season: Spring through summer.

When to plant: Set transplants when available. Cold- and heat-tolerant zones 5–9.

Light: Sunny to half-shady.

Soil: Humusy, well drained, moist.

Fertilizer: 14-14-14 or 5-10-5.

Pruning: Cut back hard in early spring; new shoots form graceful, vigorous bushes with plenty of blooms.

Propagation: Take cuttings spring through summer.

Uses: Beds, borders, specimen, containers, cottage gardens.

ITEA
(eye-TEE-ah)
Holly-leaf Itea; Sweetspire

SAXIFRAGACEAE; saxifrage family

Height/habit: Deciduous, as with sweetspire (*I. virginica*), and evergreen, as with holly-leaf itea (*I. ilicifolia*), shrubs or small trees, 8–18 ft.(2.4–5.5 m.) high/wide.

Leaves: Hollylike in holly-leaf itea, to 4 in. (10 cm.) long; finely toothed, to 3 in. (7.5 cm.) long, in sweetspire, turning brilliant red in fall.

Flowers: Tiny, growing in drooping clusters to 1 ft. (30 cm.) long in holly-leaf tea; upright to 6 in. (15 cm.) long and fragrant in sweetspire; white to greenish white.

Season: Summer.

When to plant: Set transplants when available. Cold- and heat-tolerant zones 5–9.

Light: Sunny to shady.

Soil: Well drained, moist.

Fertilizer: 14-14-14 or 5-10-5.

Pruning: Little needed except to remove winter-damaged growth in spring.

Propagation: Divide in spring or take softwood cuttings in summer; sow seeds fall through spring.

Uses: Beds; borders; background; woodland, wild, or cottage gardens; cutting.

KALMIA
(KAL-mee-ah)

Mountain Laurel; Calico Bush

ERICACEAE; heath family

Height/habit: *K. latifolia*, known as both mountain laurel and calico bush, an evergreen shrub, 6–8 ft. (1.8–2.4 m.) high/wide, eventually thicket-forming, to 15 ft. (4.5 m.) high/wide.

Leaves: Elliptic, glossy, 2–5 in. (5–12.5 cm.) long; warning: poisonous if ingested.
Flowers: Cupped, starry, to 1 in. (2.5 cm.) across, appearing in showy, terminal clusters; white, pink, rose, red, or maroon; often bi-colored.
Season: Late spring through early summer; foliage attractive all year.

When to plant: Set transplants when available. Cold- and heat-tolerant zones 4–8; marginally in zone 9 if climate is not too hot and humid in the summer and soil not too alkaline.
Light: Partly sunny to partly shady.
Soil: Humusy, well drained, moist, acidic.
Fertilizer: 14-14-14 timed-release; chelated iron in case of chlorosis (yellowed leaves with green veins).
Pruning: Only cut to remove dead wood or for flower arrangements.

Propagation: Layer spring through summer; sow seeds fall through winter; green-wood cuttings under glass winter through spring.
Uses: Borders; massed plantings; cottage, shade, woodland, or wild gardens; cutting.

KERRIA
(KEHR-ee-ah)

Japanese Rose; Variegated Kerria

ROSACEAE; rose family

Height/habit: Deciduous shrub, roselike but unarmed, gracefully rounded or fountain form, 5–8 ft. (1.5–2.4 m.) high/wide.
Leaves: Simple ovals, often toothed, to 4 in. (10 cm.) long; mixed pleasingly with white in the variegated kerrias: *K. japonica* 'Picta,' *K. j.* 'Superba,' and *K. j.* 'Variegata.'
Flowers: Resemble roses, as common name implies, to 2 in. (5 cm.) across; single (as with Japanese rose, *K. japonica*) or double (as with double Japanese rose, *K. j.* 'Pleniflora'); yellow.
Season: Spring, sporadically in summer. Bare twigs bright green in the winter landscape.

When to plant: Set transplants when available. Cold- and heat-tolerant zones 4–9.
Light: Sunny to half-shady.
Soil: Humusy, well drained, moist.
Fertilizer: 14-14-14 timed-release or rose fertilizer.
Pruning: Immediately after flowering, cut out as much old wood as possible, back to strong new shoots, even if this means pruning to the ground. Remove completely green shoots from variegated sorts.
Propagation: Take softwood cuttings in summer, hardwood cuttings fall through winter; layer or divide roots in spring.
Uses: Beds, borders, informal hedge, wild garden, cutting.

KIRENGESHOMA
(kihr-en-geh-SHOW-mah)

Kirengeshoma

SAXIFRAGACEAE; saxifrage family

Height/habit: *K. palmata* an herbaceous perennial 3–4 ft. (1.2 m.) high/wide that gives the garden effect of a deciduous shrub.

Leaves: Palmately lobed, toothed, to 9 in. (22.5 cm.) long on purplish stems.

Flowers: Nodding, trumpet-shaped, growing in terminal and axillary cymes, to 5 in. (12.5 cm.) long; yellow.

Season: Mid- to late summer.

When to plant: Set transplants when available, ideally in spring. Cold- and heat-tolerant zones 6–8.

Light: Half sunny to half shady.

Soil: Humusy, well drained, moist.

Fertilizer: 14-14-14 timed-release.

Pruning: Remove all dead parts or cut to the ground in early spring; flowers appear on new shoots.

Propagation: Divide roots or sow seeds in spring.

Uses: Beds; borders; specimen; shade, wild, or cottage gardens.

KOELREUTERIA
(kel-roo-TEHR-ee-ah)

Golden-rain Tree; Flamegold-rain Tree

SAPINDACEAE; soapberry family

Height/habit: Deciduous trees, 15–40 ft. (4.5–12.1 m.) high/wide. Especially rewarding to grow are *K. bipinnata* and *K. paniculata*, both called golden-rain tree, as well as flamegold-rain tree (*K. elegans*).
Leaves: Pinnate, 1–2 ft. (30–61 cm.) long; oval leaflets, sometimes toothed.
Flowers: Terminal panicles, 1–1.5 ft. (30–45 cm.) long; yellow; fragrant. Followed by long-lasting seed capsules that turn rose, dark red, pinkish bronze, or chartreuse.
Season: Flowers in summer, decorative seed capsules in fall.

When to plant: Set transplants when available. *S. paniculata* cold- and heat-tolerant zones 6–9, the others zones 7–8 to 10.
Light: Sunny.
Soil: Well drained, moist to on the dry side; drought-tolerant when established.
Fertilizer: 14-14-14 timed-release at planting; 5-10-5 before flowering.
Pruning: Remove all dead wood and shape late winter through early spring.
Propagation: Sow seeds spring through summer; transplant self-sown seedlings in spring.
Uses: Light shade, street, terrace, lawn; for screening if planted thicket-style.

LABURNUM
(lab-BURN-um)

Golden-chain Tree

LEGUMINOSAE; pea family

Height/habit: Ornamental deciduous shrubs to 15–20 ft. (4.5–6 m.). Trained as single-trunked trees, grow to 30 ft. (9 m.) high. Excellent choices are common golden-chain tree (*L. anagyroides*) and Voss hybrid golden-chain tree (*L. x watereri* 'Vossii').
Leaves: Cloverlike, to 3 in. (7.5 cm.) long.
Flowers: Wisterialike clusters, 8–15 in. (20–38 cm.) long; yellow.
Season: Late spring through summer.
When to plant: Set transplants when available. Cold- and heat-tolerant zones 5–7.

Light: Sunny to half-shady; protect from afternoon sun in hotter climates.
Soil: Well drained, moist.
Fertilizer: 14-14-14 timed-release at planting, 5-10-5 thereafter.
Pruning: Remove suckers faithfully if training to single-trunk tree-form standard. Late winter through early spring remove any dead or damaged growth.
Propagation: Sow seeds in fall.
Uses: Borders, background, espalier, arbor, bonsai.

LAGERSTROEMIA
(lay-gur-STREEM-ee-ah)

Crape Myrtle

LYTHRACEAE; loosestrife family

Height/habit: *L. indica* a deciduous shrub or small tree, to
20–35 ft. (6–10.5 m.) high/wide.
Dwarf types to 3 ft. (1 m.)
high/wide.

Leaves: Elliptic, 1–3 in.
(2.5–7.5 cm.) long; yellow to
scarlet in fall.

Flowers: Frilly, to 1 in. (2.5 cm.)
across, with prominent yellow
stamens in large, showy clusters; pink, red, rose, coral,
lavender, or white. Prompt
deadheading promotes more
bloom.

Season: Summer through
early fall.

When to plant: Set transplants
when available. Cold- and heat-
tolerant zones 7–9. Often man-
aged as container plants in
colder zones.

Light: Sunny.

Soil: Well drained, moist.

Fertilizer: 14-14-14 timed-
release initially, 5-10-5 thereafter; 30-10-10 or chelated iron
in the event of chlorosis (yellowish leaves).

Pruning: Remove all dead wood
in spring before new leaves
appear. Blooms appear on new
growth. Keep suckers and water
shoots removed from the base,
trunks, and main branches of
trees.

Propagation: Sow seeds winter
through spring; take cuttings
in summer.

Uses: Border, screen, lawn, light
shade, specimen, bonsai, containers (dwarf types), ground
cover (dwarf types).

LIGUSTRUM
(lig-GUST-rum)
Privet;
Golden Vicary

OLEACEAE; olive family

Height/habit: Deciduous, semi- to evergreen shrubs, rarely small trees, 10–15 ft. (3–4.5 m.) high/wide. Best deciduous choices include amur privet (*L. amurense*), border privet (*L. obtusifolium*), variegated privet (*L. sinense* 'Variegatum'), and golden vicary (*L.* x *vicaryi*). Glossy Chinese privet (*L. lucidum*) and wax-leaved privet (*L. japonicum*) are evergreen.

Leaves: Ovate to elliptic, 2–4 in. (5–10 cm.) long; variegated silvery white or golden yellow in some selections.

Flowers: Very small in dense panicles; white; unpleasantly scented.

Season: Flowers in spring or summer.

When to plant: Set transplants when available. Cold- and heat-tolerant zones 5–7 to 9–10.

Light: Sunny to shady.

Soil: Moist, well drained.

Fertilizer: 14-14-14 timed-release.

Pruning: Formal privet hedges need clipping several times each season. Specimens need little pruning except to remove dead twigs and branches.

Propagation: Take cuttings spring through summer; sow seeds in fall; plant also grows from self-sown seedlings.

Uses: Clipped or informal hedges, screens, borders, shade, seaside and city gardens, topiary, bonsai.

LINDERA
(lin-DEER-ah)

Spicebush
LAURACEAE; laurel family

Height/habit: *L. obtusiloba* deciduous shrub to 15 ft. (4.5 m.) high by one-third to one-half as wide. All parts have a spicy fragrance.

Leaves: Broad ovals, to 5 in. (12.5 cm.) across; fall color is clear yellow.

Flowers: Tiny, in dense clusters; male (staminate) and female (pistillate) on separate plants; greenish yellow.

Season: Flowers early spring, before the leaves; oblong scarlet berries persist on branches of female plant after leaves are gone.

When to plant: Set transplants when available. Larger plants intolerant of root disturbance. Cold- and heat-tolerant zones 6–9.

Light: Sunny (cooler regions) to partly shaded.

Soil: Well drained, moist.

Fertilizer: 5-10-5 or 14-14-14 timed-release.

Pruning: Remove dead wood in spring.

Propagation: Take softwood cuttings spring through summer; sow newly ripe seeds fall through winter.

Uses: Borders, background, accent, shade, butterfly and wild gardens, cutting.

LIRIODENDRON
(lihr-ee-oh-DEN-dron)

Tulip Tree
MAGNOLIACEAE; magnolia family

Height/habit: *L. tulipifera* a fast-growing deciduous tree, 60–80 ft. (18–24 m.) high, spreading to 40 ft. (12.1 m.) in a pyramidal crown.

Leaves: Lyre-shaped, 5–6 in. (12.5–15 cm.) long/wide; bright yellow-green, turning yellow or yellow-brown in fall.

Flowers: Tulip-shaped, to 2 in. (5 cm.) across; yellowish green with orange at the base; often not appearing until the tree is 10 years old.

Season: Flowers late spring.

When to plant: Set container transplants when available, ideally in spring. Avoid root disturbance. Cold- and heat-tolerant zones 4–9.

Light: Sunny.

Soil: Well drained, moist.

Fertilizer: 14-14-14 timed-release.

Pruning: Remove dead wood in spring; remove suckers from the base or water shoots from any branch in summer.

Propagation: Layer or graft cultivars spring through summer; sow seeds fall through winter.

Uses: Shade; lawn; roadside; butterfly garden; spreading roots discourage gardening under tulip tree.

MAGNOLIA
(mag-NO-lee-ah)

Cucumber Tree; Ear-leaved Umbrella Tree; Bull Bay; White Yulan; Magnolia

MAGNOLIACEAE; magnolia family

Height/habit: Ornamental shrubs to large trees, deciduous or evergreen, 10–80 ft. (3–24 m.). Noteworthy deciduous species include cucumber tree (*M. acuminata*), ear-leaved umbrella tree (*M. fraseri*), white yulan (*M. denudata*), star magnolia (*M. kobus* var. *stellata*), large-leaved cucumber tree (*M. macrophylla*), Siebold magnolia (*M. sieboldii*), and saucer magnolia (*M.* x *soulangiana*). Bull bay (*M. grandiflora*) is evergreen.

Leaves: Entire, often glossy, variously ovate, elliptic, lanceolate, obovate, or oblanceolate, 6–36 in. (15–90 cm.) long.

Flowers: Cups, saucers, or stars; 3–12 in. (7.5–30 cm.) across; pink, red, white, rose, or yellow; fragrant.

Season: Spring or summer.

When to plant: Set transplants when available. Cold- and heat-tolerant zones 5–6 to 9.

Light: Sunny to half-shady.

Soil: Well drained, moist, acidic.

Fertilizer: 14-14-14 timed-release; chelated iron to treat chlorosis (yellowish foliage).

Pruning: After flowering, remove any unwanted growth, usually taking the branch to the basal collar at its point of origination.

Propagation: Sow seeds or take hardwood cuttings fall through winter; take softwood cuttings in summer.

Uses: Specimen, lawn, garden, shade, espalier, bonsai, cutting.

MAHONIA
(mah-HOH-nee-ah)

Oregon Grape; Japanese Mahonia

BERBERIDACEAE; barberry family

Height/habit: Upright broadleaf evergreen shrubs, 3–10 ft. (1–3 m.) high/wide. *M. aquifolium* and *M. bealei*, both called Oregon grape, as well as Japanese mahonia (*M. japonica*), recommended species.

Leaves: Pinnate, spiny-toothed, 3–16 in. (7.5–40 cm.) long.

Flowers: Small in drooping racemes, 3–6 in. (7.5–15 cm.) long; yellow; fragrant.

Season: Midspring to early summer; showy bluish to purplish black fruit fall through winter.

When to plant: Set transplants when available. Cold- and heat-tolerant zones 6–9.

Light: Partly sunny to partly shady.

Soil: Humusy, well drained, moist, acidic.

Fertilizer: 14-14-14 timed-release; chelated iron to treat chlorosis (yellowish foliage).

Pruning: Little needed; remove dead growth late winter through spring. Bare branches extending awkwardly may be removed to the ground at the same time.

Propagation: Layer or take suckers spring through summer; sow seeds or take hardwood cuttings fall through winter.

Uses: Borders, informal hedge, specimen, shade and Japanese gardens, containers.

MALUS
(MAY-luss)

Crab Apple
ROSACEAE; rose family

Height/habit: Deciduous shrubs or small trees, 15–45 ft. (4.5–13.6 m.) high. Fine choices are Arnold crab apple (*M.* x *arnoldiana*), carmine crab apple (*M.* x *atrosanguinea*); Siberian crab apple (*M. baccata*), Japanese flowering crab apple (*M. floribunda*), common apple (*M. pumila* and *M. sylvestris*), cherry crab apple (*M.* x *robusta*), and Sargent crab apple (*M. sargentii*).

Leaves: Serrate- or smooth-edged, ovate or elliptic, 1–4 in. (2.5–10 cm.) long.
Flowers: Cupped or saucerlike, single or double, about 1 in. (2.5 cm.) across, growing in clusters; pink, white, rose, red, or crimson; some fragrant. Followed by edible or inedible though highly decorative fruits, from brightest red to golden yellow.
Season: Flowers in spring, light green foliage in summer; brightly colored fruit in fall, lasting well into winter on the ornamentals.
When to plant: Set transplants when available. Cold- and heat-tolerances zones 3–5 to 8; may succeed zone 9.

Light: Sunny.
Soil: Well drained, moist.
Fertilizer: 14-14-14 timed-release initially, 5-10-5 thereafter.
Pruning: Cut back after winter but before buds swell. Remove dead wood and shorten laterals by one-third on 2-year-old trees.
Propagation: Grow species from seeds sown fall through winter; grow named selections by grafting on a suitably related stock winter through spring.
Uses: Lawn, border, specimen, shade, orchard, espalier, bonsai, cutting.

MITRIOSTIGMA
(mit-ree-oh-STIG-mah)
African Gardenia
RUBIACEAE; madder family

Height/habit: *M. axillare* an upright evergreen shrub, 3–5 ft. (1–1.5 m.) high/wide.

Leaves: Elliptic, to 4 in. (10 cm.) long; dark green.

Flowers: Funnelform, 5-lobed, 3 or more together, borne at the leaf axils, to .5 in. (1.25 cm.) wide; white blushed bronzy pink on the outside; fragrant.

Season: Everblooming in moderate to warm climates with night lows of 50–60°F (10–15°C), days 70°F (21°C) or higher.

When to plant: Set transplants when available. Cold- and heat-tolerant zones 9 and warmer; elsewhere maintain as a container plant, placing outdoors in warm weather.

Light: Half-sunny to half-shady.

Soil: Humusy, well drained, moist.

Fertilizer: 30-10-10 applied with water; 14-14-14 timed-release.

Pruning: Prune at any time to remove dead wood—especially spring or summer to encourage branching.

Propagation: Take cuttings in spring or summer.

Uses: Cottage garden, border, containers.

NANDINA
(nan-DEE-nah)

Heavenly Bamboo

BERBERIDACEAE; barberry family

Height/habit: *N. domestica* an evergreen shrub 1–8 ft. (30–240 cm.) high; canelike stems.

Leaves: Narrow, pinnate on pendulous stem; leaflets to 1.5 in. (3.7 cm.) long, reduced to threadlike forms in some selections; turning bronze or red in cold weather.

Flowers: Small, appearing in clusters, to 1 ft. (30 cm.) long; white; succeeded by bright red berries.

Season: Flowers in spring; berries fall through winter.

When to plant: Set transplants when available. Cold- and heat-tolerant zones 6–9.

Light: Sunny to shady.

Soil: Well drained, moist. Established nandinas tolerate considerable drought.

Fertilizer: 14-14-14 timed-release; chelated iron in the event of chlorosis (yellowish leaves).

Pruning: Thin out oldest stems to the base in early spring; cut out any dead growth; remove dead or winter-damaged leaves.

Propagation: Divide in spring; sow seeds in fall.

Uses: Informal hedge, borders, specimen, shade or Japanese gardens, containers, bonsai.

NERIUM
(NEER-ee-um)
Oleander
APOCYNACEAE; dogbane family

Height/habit: *N. oleander* an evergreen shrub or small tree, to 20 ft. (6 m.).

Leaves: Narrow, willowlike, 6–10 in. (15–25 cm.) long.

Flowers: Single or double trumpets, 1–2 in. (2.5–5 cm.) across, growing in showy, terminal, branching clusters; white, yellow, rose, red, coral, or salmon; some bicolored; fragrant.

Season: Spring through summer.

When to plant: Set transplants when available. Cold- and heat-tolerant zones 8–10; elsewhere grow in containers that can be moved inside for winter.

Light: Sunny.

Soil: Well drained, moist to on the dry side. Established oleanders in the ground are exceedingly tolerant of drought and vehicular air pollution.

Fertilizer: 14-14-14 timed-release; chelated iron in the event of chlorosis (yellowish leaves).

Pruning: Cut back after spring bloom or throughout the season as a means of control; flowers appear at the tips of new shoots. The sap and all other parts of the oleander plant are poisonous.

Propagation: Take cuttings spring through fall.

Uses: Beds, borders, background, screening, specimen, containers, seaside gardens, tree-form standard, informal hedge.

OSMANTHUS
(oz-MANTH-us)

Sweet Olive; Tea Olive; Orange-flowered Sweet Olive; Chinese Holly-leaved Olive

OLEACEAE; olive family

Height/habit: Evergreen shrubs and trees, 20–30 ft. (6–9 m.).

Leaves: Oval-shaped in sweet olive, also called tea olive (*O. fragrans*), to 4 in. (10 cm.) long; hollylike, elliptic to oblong and 2–3 in. (5–7.5 cm.) long in Chinese holly-leaved olive (*O. heterophyllus*).

Flowers: Small, to .5 in. (1.25 cm.), growing in clusters at the leaf axils; white to creamy; fragrant. Orange-flowered sweet olive (*O. f. forma aurantiacus*) particularly beautiful.

Season: Fall through winter through spring.

When to plant: Set transplants when available. Cold- and heat-tolerant zones 7–8 to 10. Elsewhere grow as container specimen that can be wintered in a cool place protected from hard freezing.

Light: Sunny to half-sunny.

Soil: Well drained, moist.

Fertilizer: 14-14-14 timed-release.

Pruning: Remove any dead parts and shape tree late winter through spring; formal hedges and topiaries may require several shearings each growing season.

Propagation: Take cuttings of half-ripe wood in late summer.

Uses: Specimen, fragrance gardens (sweet olive), clipped hedge (Chinese holly-leaved olive), topiary, espalier, containers, bonsai.

OXYDENDRUM
(oxy-DEN-drum)
Sourwood;
Sorrel Tree
ERICACEAE; heath family

Height/habit: *O. arboreum*, called both sourwood and sorrel tree, is deciduous and slow-growing, reaching 50–60 ft. (15.1–18.2 m.).
Leaves: Oblong to lanceolate, to 8 in. (20 cm.) long; outstanding fall color.
Flowers: Small, growing in pendulous panicles, 8–10 in. (20–25 cm.) long; white; fragrant. Succeeded by dried silvery capsules, decorative fall through winter.
Season: An outstanding year-round performer.
When to plant: Set transplants when available. Cold- and heat-tolerant zones 5–9.
Light: Sunny to half-shady.
Soil: Well drained, moist.
Fertilizer: 14-14-14 timed-release.
Pruning: Little needed beyond routine maintenance.
Propagation: Sow seeds fall through winter.
Uses: Specimen, lawn, street, shade gardens.

PACHYSANDRA
(pak-iss-SAND-rah)
Allegheny Spurge;
Japanese Spurge
BUXACEAE; boxwood family

Height/habit: Evergreen ground covers, 6–12 in. (15–30 cm.) high, spreading to form dense cover if rooted cuttings or divisions are set on 8-in. (20-cm.) centers. Best choices are Allegheny spurge (*P. procumbens*) and Japanese spurge (*P. terminalis*).
Leaves: Obovate, toothed above the middle, 2–4 in. (5–10 cm.) long, clustered at the tips.
Flowers: Inconspicuous, growing in short spikes 1 in. (2.5 cm.) long; greenish white. Succeeded by white berries.

Season: Foliage attractive most seasons.
When to plant: Set transplants when available. Water well to establish. Cold- and heat-tolerant zones 4–9.
Light: Half-sunny to shady.
Soil: Humusy, well drained, moist.
Fertilizer: 14-14-14 timed-release.
Pruning: Prune only to remove dead growth at any time.
Propagation: Divide in spring; take cuttings in summer.
Uses: Ground cover under trees, on banks, around large shrubs.

PAULOWNIA
(pow-LOH-nee-ah)

Empress Tree

SCROPHULARIACEAE; figwort family

Height/habit: *P. tomentosa* a deciduous tree, 40–60 ft. (12.1–18.2 m) high.
Leaves: Broadly oval, 3-lobed, to 1 ft. (30 cm.) or more; densely matted beneath with short, woolly hairs.
Flowers: Lobed pouches, to 2 in. (5 cm.) across, in showy pyramidal panicles to 1 ft. (30 cm.) long; violet-blue.
Season: Spring, as leaves begin to unfold.

When to plant: Set transplants when available. Cold- and heat-tolerant zones 6–9.
Light: Sunny to half-sunny.
Soil: Humusy, well drained, moist.
Fertilizer: 14-14-14 timed-release.
Pruning: Remove any dead wood in early spring; for any major cutting, wait until immediately after flowering. If frozen to the ground, cut back hard in spring; new shoots will reach 12 ft. (3.6 m.) that season, with leaves to 1.5 ft. (45 cm.) across.
Propagation: Sow seeds or take root cuttings in spring.
Uses: Specimen, lawn, garden, park.

PERNETTYA
(per-NETT-ee-ah)

Chilean Myrtle

ERICACEAE; heath family

Height/habit: *P. mucronata* an evergreen shrub, 2–3 ft. (61–90 cm.) high/wide.
Leaves: Densely set on much-branched shrub, oval-shaped, to 1 in. (2.5 cm.) long; lightly toothed, tipped with sharp spine.
Flowers: Numerous, nodding, about .25 in. (.63 cm.) long; white, pink, or red.
Season: Spring through early summer.
When to plant: Set transplants when available. Narrowly cold- and heat-tolerant zones 7–8; ideal in cool, moist regions, free of temperature extremes.

Light: Sunny.
Soil: Humusy, well drained, moist, acidic.
Fertilizer: 14-14-14 timed-release; chelated iron in response to chlorosis (yellowish foliage).
Pruning: Little needed; remove any long, straggly growths when full of berries so they can be enjoyed indoors.
Propagation: Take cuttings of half-ripe wood or suckers or layer in summer; sow seeds in fall.
Uses: Specimen, border, rock gardens.

PHILADELPHUS
(fil-ad-DELF-us)
Mock Orange
SAXIFRAGACEAE; saxifrage family

Height/habit: Deciduous shrubs with curving or drooping branches, 4–12 ft. (1.2–3.6 m.) high/wide. Good choices are common mock orange (*P. coronarius*), *P. lewisii* 'Waterton,' and dwarf mock orange (*P. microphyllus*).

Leaves: Oval, lanceolate, or elliptic, 1–5 in. (2.5–12.5 cm.) long.

Flowers: Cup- or saucer-shaped, single or double, 1–2 in. (2.5–5 cm.) across, single or clustered; white; some fragrant.

Season: Late spring early summer.

When to plant: Set transplants when available. Cold- and heat-tolerant zones 4–9.

Light: Sunny.

Soil: Well drained, moist.

Fertilizer: 14-14-14 timed-release.

Pruning: After flowering, prune to shape; new wood will produce next year's flowers.

Propagation: Sow seeds in spring; take softwood cuttings or layer in spring.

Uses: Borders, screening, informal hedge, background, specimen.

PHOTINIA
(foh-TIN-ee-ah)

Photinia

ROSACEAE; rose family

Height/habit: Deciduous
(*P. villosa*) or evergreen
(*P. glabra* and *serrulata*) grow
to size of shrubs or trees,
8–30 ft. (2.4–9 m.).

Leaves: Oblong, glossy, 3–8 in.
(7.5–20 cm.) long; tips red as
new growth develops.

Flowers: Small, growing in
clusters, 4–6 in. (10–15 cm.)
long; white; followed by bright
red fruit.

Season: Year-round performers.

When to plant: Set transplants
when available. Cold- and heat-
tolerant zones 5–7 to 9–10; use
locally adapted species.

Light: Sunny to half-sunny.

Soil: Humusy, well drained,
moist.

Fertilizer: 14-14-14 timed-
release.

Pruning: Little needed. Cut
back long straggly branches
on *P. villosa* in fall. For *P.
glabra*, cut back after flowering in spring; this promotes
young red-tipped leaves.

Propagation: Sow seeds, take
softwood cuttings, or layer
spring through summer.

Uses: Foliage effect, specimen,
lawn, landscape, Japanese
garden, screening, hedge,
containers.

PIERIS
(PYE-er-iss)

Andromeda

ERICACEAE; heath family

Height/habit: Erect, broadleaf evergreen shrubs or small trees, 10–30 ft. (3–9 m.), often much smaller. Recommended are mountain andromeda (*P. floribunda*), scarlet andromeda (*P. forestii*), and Japanese andromeda (*P. japonica*).

Leaves: Obovate to oblanceolate, 3–6 in. (7.5–15 cm.) long; whorled, glossy green, leathery; brilliant red, pink, or glowing burgundy-cordovan in the new growth of some cultivars.

Flowers: Small, waxy, .5-in (1.25-cm.) urns, growing in pendulous, long-lasting clusters, to 6 in. (15 cm.) long; white.

Season: Spring from budding time.

When to plant: Set transplants when available. Cold- and heat-tolerant zones 5–8.

Light: Partly sunny to partly shady.

Soil: Humusy, well drained, moist, acidic.

Fertilizer: 14-14-14 timed-release; chelated iron in the event of chlorosis (yellowish foliage).

Pruning: Little needed except for spring cleanup; later, cut out only odd branches that stick out beyond the shrub's outline.

Propagation: Take cuttings or layer in summer; sow seeds in fall.

Uses: Borders, screen, informal hedge, specimen, shade, woodland garden, containers, bonsai.

PINUS
(PEE-nus)

Pine

PINACEAE; pine family

Height/habit: Evergreen trees bearing true cones, to 100 ft. (30 cm.) high/wide. *P. densiflora* 'Pendula' particularly noteworthy.

Leaves: Needlelike or overlapping scales 2–4 in. (5–10 cm.) long.

Flowers: Inconspicuous, except for the large amount of pollen produced by some.

Season: Flowers in spring; cones grow in summer, mature in fall. Foliage attractive in all seasons, often taking on a different hue during coldest weather.

When to plant: Set transplants when available. Cold- and heat-tolerant most zones, depending on individual adaptability; it is a wise policy with conifers to purchase from a local nursery known to sell only locally adapted species.

Light: Sunny.

Soil: Well drained, moist; some drought-tolerant when established.

Fertilizer: 14-14-14 timed release.

Pruning: Trim dead wood at any time. Cuttings for house garlanding can often comprise entire pruning for the year. Hedge can be clipped after the first flush of new growth in spring.

Propagation: Take cuttings of horticultural varieties fall through winter; alternatively, sow seeds in protected frames outdoors before winter freeze, for germination in a year or two.

Uses: Beds, borders, background, hedgerow, windbreak, ground cover, espalier, bonsai, cutting.

PITTOSPORUM
(pit-TOSP-or-um)

Japanese Pittosporum

PITTOSPORACEAE; pittosporum family

Height/habit: *P. tobira* a broadleaf evergreen shrub that branches naturally into a layered shrub, to 10 ft. (3 m.) high/wide.

Leaves: Whorled, leathery, lustrous, to 4 in. (10 cm.) long; white-and-silver variegation in some.

Flowers: To .5 in. (1.25 cm.) across, growing in clusters; white or pale yellow; fragrant.

Season: Late spring through early summer.

When to plant: Set transplants when available. Water deeply to establish. Cold- and heat-tolerant zones 8–10.

Light: Sunny to half-sunny.

Soil: Humusy, well drained, moist, acidic.

Fertilizer: 14-14-14 timed-release.

Pruning: Little needed, except for spring cleanup; sometimes sheared or cut back as a means of control or to encourage more branching.

Propagation: Take green-wood cuttings in late summer.

Uses: Informal hedge, screening, Japanese garden, lawn specimen.

PLUMERIA
(ploo-MEER-ee-ah)

Singapore Plumeria; Frangipani

APOCYNACEAE; dogbane family

Height/habit: Evergreen Singapore plumeria (*P. obtusa*) or deciduous frangipani (*P. rubra*) grow to size of shrubs or trees, 6–12 ft. (1.8–3.6 m.) high/wide—more in zone 10, where they can live in the ground all year.

Leaves: Oblong to lanceolate, 4–6 in. (10–15 cm.) long.

Flowers: Tubular, 1–3 in. (2.5–7.5 cm.) across, in clusters at the tips; from white and cream through pale to dark yellow; also reds, pinks, and intriguing blends; fragrant.

Season: Summer through fall.

When to plant: Set transplants when available. Cold- and heat-tolerant zones 9–12; suited to container culture in colder regions.

Light: Sunny.

Soil: Well drained; moist to on the dry side in the active season, on the dry side while semi-dormant fall through winter.

Fertilizer: 5-10-5 or fertilizer labeled for Chinese hibiscus.

Pruning: None required.

Propagation: Take cuttings spring through summer; sow seeds in spring.

Uses: Borders, accent, specimen, containers (large and heavy to counterbalance the plumeria's tendency toward top-heaviness).

PODOCARPUS
(poh-doh-KARP-us)

Southern Yew; Japanese Yew

PODOCARPACEAE; podocarpus family

Height/habit: *P. macrophyllus*, known as Southern yew and Japanese yew, is evergreen, upright, and columnar, growing to 20 ft. (6 m.) high x 7 ft. (2.1 m.) across; specimen trees to 50 ft. (15 m.) high.
Leaves: Narrow, to 4 in. (10 cm.) long; new light green leaves age to dark green.
Flowers: Inconspicuous.
Season: Foliage attractive all year.
When to plant: Set transplants when available. Cold- and heat-tolerant zones 8–10.

Light: Sunny to partly shady.
Soil: Humusy, well drained, moist.
Fertilizer: 14-14-14 timed-release.
Pruning: Clip hedges after the first flush of spring growth, again if needed in a long season. Little needed for podocarpus in general, except to remove dead or broken branches as they appear.
Propagation: Sow seeds or transplant self-sown seedlings spring through summer.
Uses: Hedge, screening, vertical accent, containers, espalier, bonsai.

PONCIRUS
(pon-SYE-rus)

Hardy Orange

RUTACEAE; rue family

Height/habit: *P. trifoliata* a deciduous, spiny shrub or tree growing to 15 ft. (4.5 m.) high.
Leaves: Trifoliate and citruslike, to 3 in. (7.5 cm.) long.
Flowers: Appearing before the leaves and growing to 2 in. (5 cm.) across; white; fragrant.
Season: Flowers in spring; apricotlike fruit in fall; exudes a wonderful scent when picked on a cool fall day, then brought into a warm room.
When to plant: Set transplants when available. Cold- and heat-tolerant zones 5–9.
Light: Sunny.
Soil: Humusy, well drained, moist, acidic.

Fertilizer: 14-14-14 timed-release.
Pruning: Maintain overall shape with minimal cutting; hedges can be clipped late spring through early summer; tree-form standards sheared 2 or 3 times from spring to midsummer.
Propagation: Sow newly ripened seeds fall through winter; alternatively, transplant self-sown seedlings at any season, taking care to coddle the roots until they are re-established.
Uses: Impenetrable hedgerow or clipped hedge, tree-form standard, specimen, cottage and country gardens.

POPULUS
(POP-yew-lus)

Poplar;
Quaking Aspen

SALICACEAE; willow family

Height/habit: Deciduous trees, 50–100 ft. (15–30 m.) or more, most needing a large space where the water-thirsty roots will not overtake the pavement or cultivated garden. Lombardy poplar (*P. nigra* var. *italica*) lives just 25 years.

Leaves: Oval to rounded, linear, or lobed, 3–6 in. (7.5–15 cm.) long; bright yellow fall color in some.

Flowers: Catkins appear in spring before leaves; 2–6 in. (5–15 cm.) long, male (staminate) and female (pistillate) on separate trees.

Season: Attractive in all seasons.

When to plant: Set transplants when available. Cold- and heat-tolerant zones 2–4 to 8. White poplar (*P. alba*) ranges zones 3–8, while columnar poplar (*P.* x *berolinensis*) and cottonwood poplar (*P. deltoides*) only to zone 3; quaking aspen (*P. tremuloides*) to zone 2. Canadian poplar (*P.* x *canadensis*) to zone 4.

Light: Sunny.

Soil: Moist, well drained.

Fertilizer: 14-14-14 timed-release.

Pruning: Except for dead or damaged wood, do cuts for formulative or corrective training of tree in winter while it is dormant.

Propagation: Take cuttings spring through summer; sow newly harvested seeds or transplant self-sown seedlings in fall.

Uses: Windbreaks, screening, large landscape specimen.

PRUNUS
(PROON-us)

Almond; Apricot; Cherry; Plum; Cherry Laurel

ROSACEAE; rose family

Height/habit: Usually deciduous woody plants, 4–60 ft. (1.2–18.2 m.). Among favorites are flowering almond (*P. triloba*), Japanese cherry (*P. serruluta*), Japanese plum (*P. salicina*), peach (*P. persica*), Japanese fragrant apricot (*P. mume*), beach plum (*P. maritima*), cherry laurel (*P. laurocerasus*), plum (*P. domestica*), sour cherry (*P. cerasus*), flowering plum (*P. cerasifera* var. *atropurpurea*, sweet cherry (*P. avium*), and almond (*P. amygdalus*).

Leaves: Alternate, simple, toothed, 2–6 in. (5–15 cm.) long; copper- and purple-leaved in some varieties.

Flowers: Cupped or saucerlike, single or double, 1 in. (2.5 cm.) across; white, pink, rose, or red; some fragrant. Followed by fruit, some edible, others ornamental; yellow, red, purple, or black.

Season: Flowers in spring; fruit summer through fall.

When to plant: Set transplants when available. Cold- and heat-tolerant zones 2–6 to 8–9; best to purchase plants known to be locally adapted.

Light: Sunny.

Soil: Well drained, moist.

Fertilizer: 14-14-14 timed-release initially, 5-10-5 thereafter.

Pruning: Best done while in bloom. For flowering almonds, following flowering, cut the young wood back to within 2 or 3 buds of the old branches.

Propagate: Sow seeds fall through winter; by budding late winter through spring; cuttings under glass fall through winter.

Uses: Specimen, border, hedgerow, espalier, bonsai.

PYRACANTHA
(pye-rah-KANTH-ah)

Scarlet Firethorn

ROSACEAE; rose family

Height/habit: *P. coccinea* a variously upright or sprawling evergreen shrub, 12–15 ft. (3.6–4.5 m.) high/wide.

Leaves: Linear to oblong or lanceolate, toothed, often bristle-tipped, 1–2 in. (2.5–5 cm.) long.

Flowers: Small, growing on year-old shoots in clusters 1–2 in. (2.5–5 cm.) across; white. Followed by showy fruit colored red, golden, orange, or scarlet.

Season: Year-round performers; fruit most showy fall through early winter.

When to plant: Set transplants when available. Cold- and heat-tolerant zones 6–7 to 9. Cultivars 'Thornless' and 'Kasan' can take more cold, to zone 5.

Light: Sunny to half-shady.

Soil: Well drained, moist to on the dry side.

Fertilizer: 14-14-14 timed-release initially, rose fertilizer subsequently.

Pruning: Soon after flowering, trim and groom; tie in new espalier shoots as appropriate; cut back wayward or superfluous growth, taking care to preserve as many of the developing fruit clusters as possible. Late summer, remove secondary shoots that are obscuring the fruit clusters; direct sunlight produces the most colorful and abundant fruit. Use heavy gloves and wear sturdy clothing to protect against the pyracantha's needle-sharp thorns.

Propagation: Take half-ripe cuttings summer through fall; sow seeds fall through winter.

Uses: Impenetrable hedgerow and wildlife safe haven, screening, outstanding for espalier or bonsai.

PYRUS
(PYE-rus)

Pear

ROSACEAE; rose family

Height/habit: Large shrubs or trees, deciduous or evergreen, 30–50 ft. (9–15 m.) high/wide. Among fine choices are common pear (*P. communis*), Bradford ornamental pear (*P. calleryana* 'Bradford'), ornamental pear (*P. ussuriensis*), and evergreen pear (*P. kawakamii*).

Leaves: Long and narrow to ovate, 2–5 in. (5–12.5 cm.) long. Brilliant scarlet fall color in ornamental pear.

Flowers: Appearing before or with leaves; small, growing in showy clusters; white or near-white.

Season: Early spring.

When to plant: Set transplants when available. Cold- and heat-tolerant zones 4–5 to 8–9; evergreen pear zones 8–9. Ornamental pear hardiest of all, to zone 4.

Light: Sunny.

Soil: Well drained, moist.

Fertilizer: 14-14-14 initially, rose fertilizer subsequently.

Pruning: Remove weak or crossing branches and thin crowded growth in winter. Bonsai and espaliers require appropriate trimming later, until early summer.

Propagation: Sow seeds fall through winter; bud or graft winter through spring.

Uses: Specimen, street, lawn, garden, espalier, bonsai.

QUERCUS
(KWURK-us)

Oak

FAGACEAE; beech family

Height/habit: Evergreen and deciduous shrubs and trees, 10–100 ft. (3–30 m.). Varied choices include the deciduous species white oak (*Q. alba*), scarlet oak (*Q. coccinea*), and red oak (*Q. rubra*). Evergreen types include California live oak (*Q. agrifolia*) and live oak (*Q. virginiana*).
Leaves: Usually lobed and deeply cut, 5–9 in. (12.5–22.5 cm.) long. Outstanding fall color, some persisting into winter.
Flowers: Inconspicuous, males in a long catkin, females short and spiky.
Season: Year-round performers.

When to plant: Set transplants when available. Cold- and heat-tolerant 4–9 to 8–10; select locally adapted oaks.
Light: Sunny.
Soil: Well drained, moist. Some oaks drought-tolerant.
Fertilizer: 14-14-14 timed-release.
Pruning: Cut back in winter to guide growth, develop strong central leader, and ensure well-placed main branches; also in winter, thin out old trees to increase light on the ground; remove any winter-damaged branches in spring.
Propagation: Sow seeds spring through fall.
Uses: Specimen, street, lawn, garden, hedgerow or wind-break, seaside, screening, espalier, bonsai.

RHODODENDRON
(roh-doh-DEN-dron)

Azalea Types: Gable Hybrids, Ghent, Glenn Dale Hybrid, Indian, Knap Hill, Kurume, and, Mollis

ERICACEAE; heath family

Height/habit: Deciduous or evergreen shrubs, 3–8 ft. (1–2.4 m.) high/wide.
Leaves: Smooth-margined, from fingernail-sized to 3–5 in. (7.5–12.5 cm.) long, whorled into clusters at the branch tips.
Flowers: Funnel-shaped, single, double, or hose-in-hose, 1–3 in. (2.5–7.5 cm.) across, appearing in showy clusters; most colors; some fragrant.
Season: Primarily spring but in some climates azaleas bloom nearly every day of the year.

When to plant: Set transplants when available. Cold- and heat-tolerant zones 5–9.
Light: Sunny to half-shady.
Soil: Humusy, well drained, moist, acidic.
Fertilizer: 14-14-14 timed-release; chelated iron in the event of chlorosis (yellowish leaves).
Pruning: Little needed, except to remove weak or dead wood; cut back immediately after flowering to control or direct growth. Since azaleas bud and grow out in a 5-spoke radial pattern, routinely pinching back 2 out of the 5 results in a pleasing layered effect.
Propagation: Take cuttings or sow seeds spring through summer.
Uses: Beds, borders, screening, informal hedge, specimen, shade, wild and cottage gardens, tree-form standard, bonsai.

RHODODENDRON
(rho-doh-DEN-dron)

Rhododendron Hybrid Types: Catawba, Caucasian, Fortune, and Griffithianum

ERICACEAE; heath family

Height/habit: Broadleaf evergreen shrubs or small trees, 10–30 ft. (3–9 m.) high/wide.
Leaves: Oblong to obovate, leathery, glossy, to 10 in. (25 cm.) long, whorled toward the branch tips; reverses covered with brown hairs in some.
Flowers: Bell-shaped, to 3 in. (7.5 cm.) across, in showy clusters; most colors. Deadheading immediately after bloom promotes more flowering the next year.
Season: Spring through early summer.

When to plant: Set transplants when available. Cold- and heat-tolerant zones 4–8; selected cultivars zone 9 without long, hot, humid summers.
Light: Half-sunny to half-shady.
Soil: Humusy, well drained, moist, acidic.
Fertilizer: 14-14-14 timed-release; chelated iron in the event of chlorosis (yellowish leaves).
Pruning: Little needed except routine spring tidying. During winter through early spring, old shrubs can be rejuvenated by cutting branches back hard to old wood, resulting in more vigorous flowering specimens 2 or 3 years later.
Propagation: Take 2–3-in.-(5–7.5-cm.-) long green-wood cuttings in early summer; cut off up to two-thirds of each leaf to reduce transpiration.
Uses: Borders, screening, informal hedge, shade and wild gardens, public gardens, and parks.

ROSA
(ROH-zah)

Rose

ROSACEAE; rose family

Height/habit: Deciduous, thorny shrubs, from ground covers to climbers, 1–30 ft. (30–900 cm. [9 m.]) high/wide.
Leaves: Many pinnate, 3–6 in. (7.5–15 cm.) long; new shoots reddish bronze in some.
Flowers: Cup- or saucer-shaped, single or double, 1–6 in. (2.5–15 cm.) across, borne singly or in clusters; all colors except true blue; many fragrant; followed by colorful hips in some species. Deadheading recommended for modern hybrids. Cluster-flowered landscape roses need little attention.
Season: All year in mild climates; summer through fall elsewhere. Note: Some roses bloom once a year; others intermittently or constantly.

When to plant: Set transplants when available. Cold- and heat-tolerant zones 3–5 to 8–9; important to select locally adapted roses.
Light: Sunny to half-sunny.
Soil: Well drained, moist.
Fertilizer: 14-14-14 timed-release or any rose fertilizer.
Pruning: Remove all dead wood late winter through early spring. Wait to do serious pruning on all once-a-year bloomers until they finish flowering, usually by early summer; remove to the ground some of the oldest canes to boost vigorous new shoots for next season's flowers.
Propagation: Take green-wood cuttings summer through fall; take hardwood cuttings fall through winter; sow seeds fall through winter.
Uses: Beds, borders, informal hedges, hedgerows, screening, arbors, trellises, fences, cottage gardens, containers, tree-form standards.

ROSMARINUS
(rohz-mah-RYE-nus)

Rosemary

LABIATAE; mint family

Height/habit: *R. officinalis* an evergreen shrub, variously upright, bushy, or cascading, depending on the variety, to 4–6 ft. (1.2–1.8 m.) high/wide.
Leaves: Linear, narrow, .5–1 in. (1.25–2.5 cm.) long.
Flowers: Typical mint with prominent lip, to .5 in. (1.25 cm.); blue, white, or pink.
Season: Year-round performer; flowers spring through summer or during almost any season.
When to plant: Set transplants when available. 'Arp' and 'Hilltop' cold- and heat-tolerant zones 7–9; other rosemaries zones 8–9. In Gulf Coast areas with hot, humid summers, rosemary does better if containerized and could benefit from being moved to more shade at height of summer.
Light: Sunny.
Soil: Well drained, moist to on the dry side.
Fertilizer: 14-14-14 timed-release.
Pruning: Remove dead growth and shape in spring; shearing can be repeated after the main flowering.
Propagation: Take cuttings in summer; layer spring through summer.
Uses: Beds; edging; borders; herb, cottage, and rock gardens; containers; tree-form standard; topiary; and bonsai.

ROYSTONEA
(roy-STOH-nee-ah)

Florida Royal Palm

PALMAE; palm family

Height/habit: Evergreen trees, 60–100 ft. (18–30 m.) high.
Leaves: Long plumes or fan-shaped, 1–6 ft. (30–180 cm.).
Flowers: Often in showy or curious drooping panicles; becoming brightly colored, light green, golden, or red.
Season: All-year performers.

When to plant: Set transplants when available. Cold- and heat-tolerant zones 9–10.
Light: Sunny to half-sunny.
Soil: Well drained, moist.
Fertilizer: 14-14-14 timed-release.
Pruning: Prune to remove dead parts at any time.
Propagation: Sow seeds spring through summer.
Uses: Specimen, street, or lawn tree; shade, desert, seaside, or tropical gardens.

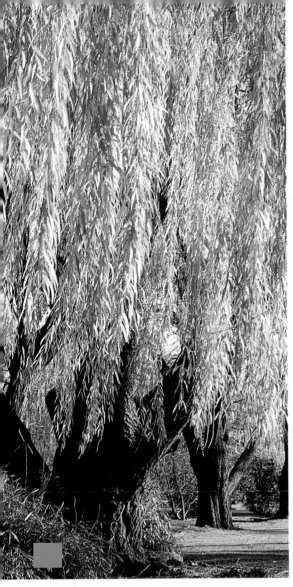

SALIX
(SAY-lix)

Willow; Purple Osier

SALICACEAE; willow family

Height/habit: Vary from deciduous shrubs to towering trees, from prostrate to 75 ft. (22.7 m.) high. Best choices include weeping willow (*S. babylonica*), white willow (*S. alba*), goat willow (*S. caprea*), pussy willow (*S. discolor*), laurel willow (*S. pentandra*), purple osier (*S. purpurea*), *S. alba* 'Vitellaniana,' and *S. sacalinensis* 'Sekka.'

Leaves: Lanceolate to oblong, 4–6 in. (10–15 cm.) long.

Flowers: Very small, in catkins, male and female on separate plants.

Season: Early spring for pussy willows; winter for those having colorful bark, such as *S. alba* 'Vitellaniana' and purple osier; weeping willows picturesque in all seasons.

When to plant: Set transplants when available. Variously cold- and heat-tolerant zones 4–5 to 8–9.

Light: Sunny.

Soil: Well drained, moist to wet.

Fertilizer: 14-14-14 timed-release.

Pruning: Prune trees while young to ensure strong leader and well-spaced branches. For kinds with colorful winter bark, cut back hard in early spring, within 1 or 2 buds of old wood. For kinds with catkins, thin out as the leaves are unfolding, cutting some of the oldest canes to the ground.

Propagation: Take green-wood cuttings in summer.

Uses: Trees as specimens in large landscapes, parks, public gardens, sides of streams or ponds; shrubs as ground cover, screening, informal hedge, specimen, borders, cutting for pussy willows or basket weaving; other types suited to bonsai.

SAMBUCUS
(sam-BEW-kus)

Elder

CAPRIFOLIACEAE; honeysuckle family

Height/habit: Deciduous shrubs and small trees, 12–15 ft. (3.6–4.5 m.) to 40 ft. (12.1 m.) high. Sweet elder (*S. canadensis*) and English golden elder (*S. racemosa* 'Plumosa-aurea') are good choices.

Leaves: Elliptic- to lance-shaped leaflets, to 6 in. (15 cm.) long.

Flowers: Very small in flat clusters to 10 in. (25 cm.) across; very lacy, large, and similar to Queen Anne's lace; white; followed by red or black fruit.

Season: Flowers spring through summer.

When to plant: Set transplants when available. Cold- and heat-tolerant zones 4–9.

Light: Sunny.

Soil: Humusy, well drained, moist.

Fertilizer: 14-14-14 timed-release.

Pruning: Prune for general maintenance in early spring; if grown for colorful leaves, cut back in spring to 1 or 2 buds from the old wood.

Propagation: Sow seeds, take cuttings or suckers, or transplant self-sown seedlings spring through summer.

Uses: Borders, specimen, background, hedgerow, screening, wild gardens.

SPIRAEA
(spye-REE-ah)
Spirea
ROSACEAE; rose family

Height/habit: Deciduous
shrubs, 2–8 ft. (61–240 cm.)
high/wide. Excellent varieties
include Japanese white spirea
(*S. albiflora*), garland spirea
(*S.* x *arguta*), Anthony Waterer
spirea (*S.* x *bumalda* 'Anthony
Waterer'), Japanese spirea
(*S. japonica* 'Rubberima'),
bridal wreath spirea
(*S. prunifolia*), and Vanhoutte
spirea (*S.* x *vanhouttei*).

Leaves: Simple or lobed,
oblong, elliptic, or lanceolate,
1–4 in. (2.5–10 cm.) long,
some toothed.

Flowers: Small, 2–4 in. (5–10
cm.) across, flat or rounded
growing in showy clusters;
white, pink, or crimson.

Season: Spring or summer.

When to plant: Set transplants
when available. Cold- and heat-
tolerant zones 4–5 to 8–9.

Light: Sunny to partly sunny.

Soil: Well drained, moist.

Fertilizer: 14-14-14 timed-
release initially, 5-10-5 subsequently.

Pruning: Prune kinds that
bloom in spring on wood from
the previous season after
flowering, cutting to evident
new shoots; for kinds that
bloom late summer on wood
produced currently, cut back in
spring to within 2 or 3 buds
from the old wood.

Propagation: Sow seeds,
take cuttings, or layer spring
through summer.

Uses: Border, informal hedge,
cottage gardens, bonsai.

STEWARTIA
(stew-ART-ee-ah)

Silky Camellia; Stewartia

THEACEAE; tea family

Height/habit: Deciduous shrubs or trees, 8–30 ft. (2.4–9 m.) high/wide. Recommended are silky camellia (*S. malacodendron*), as well as Japanese stewartia (*S. pseudocamellia*) and Chinese stewartia (*S. sinensis*).

Leaves: Alternate, simple, toothed, ovate to elliptic, 3–6 in. (7.5–15 cm.) long; fall color.
Flowers: Saucerlike, 2–4 in. (5–10 cm.) across; white with showy stamens, bluish, purple, or orange-yellow.
Season: Summer.
When to plant: Set transplants when available; disturb the roots as little as possible. Cold- and heat-tolerant zones 5–7 to 8–9.
Light: Partly sunny to partly shady.
Soil: Humusy, moist, well drained, acidic.

Fertilizer: 14-14-14 timed-release; chelated iron in the event of chlorosis (yellowish leaves).
Pruning: Little needed except for tidying up after winter.
Propagation: Sow seeds, take softwood cuttings, or layer in summer.
Uses: Borders, specimen, lawn, woodland or wild gardens, bonsai.

SYRINGA
(sihr-RIN-gah)

Lilac

OLEACEAE; olive family

Height/habit: Deciduous shrubs or small trees, 6–30 ft. (1.8–9 m.) high/wide. Gorgeous choices include Japanese tree lilac (*S. amurensis* var. *japonica*), small-leaved lilac (*S. microphylla*), lacy Persian lilac (*S. x persica* var. *laciniata*), Preston Hybrid lilac (*S. x prestoniae* 'Babella'), and classic old-fashioned lilac (*S. vulgaris*).
Leaves: Mostly simple, oval- or heart-shaped, 1–7 in. (2.5–17 cm.) long.

Flowers: Small, growing in showy panicles or loose clusters, 3–10 in. (7.5–25 cm.) long; most colors except bright yellows, reds, and oranges; fragrant.
Season: Late spring to early summer.
When to plant: Set transplants when available. Cold- and heat-tolerant zones 3–6 to 8; needs winter chilling.
Light: Sunny.
Soil: Well drained, moist, neutral to alkaline.
Fertilizer: 14-14-14 timed-release. Fireplace ashes often used as side-dressing in spring for alkalizing effect.

Pruning: Remove flower trusses as soon as they fade; remove any weak growth from the bush interior. Cut back high-growing 1-and 2-year shoots by one-half to two-thirds immediately after flowering. Rejuvenate old lilacs by cutting to the ground in early spring all weak branches. Train new shoots; may not bloom for 3 years.
Propagation: Take cuttings or layer in summer; grow from stratified seeds or graft in spring.
Uses: Borders, specimens, informal hedge, screening, cottage gardens, tree-form standard, bonsai, cutting.

TAMARIX
(TAM-ah-rix)

Athel Tamarisk; Salt Tree; Tamarisk

TAMARICACEAE; tamarisk family

Height/habit: Deciduous shrubs or trees, 15–30 ft. (1.5–9 m.) high/wide. Recommended are athel tamarix, or salt tree (*T. aphylla*), and tamarisk (*T. pentandra*).
Leaves: Alternate, scalelike, 2–3 in. (5–7.5 cm.) long.
Flowers: Feathery racemes, 1–2 in. (2.5–5 cm.) long; pink.
Season: Spring through summer through fall.
When to plant: Set transplants when available. Cold- and heat-tolerant zones 5–9.
Light: Sunny.
Soil: Well drained, moist to on the dry side; neutral to alkaline pH.
Fertilizer: 14-14-14 timed-release.
Pruning: If plant flowers in spring, cut back immediately thereafter; if it flowers late summer through fall, prune back hard in late winter. These are tough plants that can go neglected and still put on a show.
Propagation: Sow seeds or take cuttings spring through summer.
Uses: Border, specimen, screening, informal hedge, seaside garden, windbreak, bonsai.

TIBOUCHINA
(tib-ooh-KEE-nah)

Glory Bush; Princess Flower

MELASTOMACEAE; melastoma family

Height/habit: *T. urvilleana* a semievergreen shrub, 5–10 ft. (1.5–3 m.) high/wide.
Leaves: Oblong to ovate, 2–4 in. (5–10 cm.) long, with distinctive lengthwise veins and soft, hairy undersides; turning golden and scarlet in chilly but not freezing fall weather.
Flowers: Saucerlike, 2–5 in. (5–12.5 cm.) across, growing singly or in groups of 3; blue-purple with prominent pink stamens.
Season: Summer through fall.
When to plant: Set transplants when available. Cold- and heat-tolerant zones 9–10; grow as a container specimen elsewhere and protect from killing frost.
Light: Sunny.
Soil: Well drained, moist, acidic.
Fertilizer: 14-14-14 timed-release.
Pruning: Cut back hard in late winter through early spring. Flowers appear at the tips of new growth, so frequent pinching out early results in more flowering branches later.
Propagation: Take half-ripe cuttings in summer; cut the leaf tips back by half or more to reduce transpiration.
Uses: Beds, borders, cottage gardens, specimen, container, tree-form standard.

VIBURNUM
(vye-BURN-um)

Viburnum; Nannyberry; Cranberry Bush; Japanese Snowball; Black Haw

CAPRIFOLIACEAE; honeysuckle family

Height/habit: Chiefly deciduous shrubs and trees, 5–30 ft. (1.5–9 m.) high/wide. Best choices are English hybrid viburnum (*V.* x *carlcephalum*), *V.* x *carlesii*, nannyberry (*V. lentago*), European cranberry bush (*V. opulus*), Japanese snowball (*V. plicatum*), black haw (*V. prunifolium*), and American cranberry (*V. trilobum*).

Leaves: Ovate, elliptic, or 3-lobed, to 4 in. (10 cm.) long.

Flowers: Showy clusters, ball-shaped ("snowball"), fertile flowers in flat clusters surrounded by larger, sterile flowers, 3–6 in. (7.5–15 cm.) across; white, creamy, or pinkish; many are fragrant.

Season: Spring through early summer; followed by showy red fruit in many species.

When to plant: Set transplants when available. Cold- and heat-tolerant zones 3–7 to 8–10.

Light: Sunny to partly shady.

Soil: Humusy, well drained, moist.

Fertilizer: 14-14-14 timed-release.

Pruning: Little needed. If growth dense and crowded, thin out in winter.

Propagation: Grow from stratified seeds in spring; take softwood cuttings and layer in summer; take hardwood cuttings fall through winter.

Uses: Borders, specimen, informal hedge, screening, hedgerow, woodland garden.

VINCA
(VIN-kah)

Trailing Vinca; Running Myrtle

APOCYNACEAE; dogbane family

Height/habit: Creeping or trailing evergreens, 3–6 ft. (1–1.8 m.) high/wide. Trailing vinca (*V. major*) and running myrtle (*V. minor*) good choices.

Leaves: Ovate to oblong, to 2 in. (5 cm.) long; variegated silvery or gold in some varieties.
Flowers: Pinwheels, 1–2 in. (2.5–5 cm.) across; blue, white, pink, or purple.
Season: Spring.
When to plant: Set transplants when available. Running myrtle cold- and heat-tolerant to zone 4; trailing vinca zones 7–9.
Light: Sunny to shady.

Soil: Humusy, well drained, moist. Water generously to establish.
Fertilizer: 14-14-14 timed-release.
Pruning: Tidy up in spring by removing all dead growth.
Propagation: Take cuttings, divide, or layer spring through summer.
Uses: Ground cover, containers (spilling over sides).

WEIGELA
(wye-JEE-lah)

Common Weigela

CAPRIFOLIACEAE; honeysuckle family

Height/habit: *W. florida* a deciduous shrub with curving, spreading branches, 8–10 ft. (2.4–3 m.) high/wide.

Leaves: Elliptic or obovate, to 4 in. (10 cm.) long; a variegated form is cultivated.

Flowers: Funnel-shaped, about 1 in. (2.5 cm.) long, growing in compound clusters; pink, rose, rose purple, ruby red.

Season: Late spring through summer.

When to plant: Set transplants when available. Cold- and heat-tolerant zones 4–9.

Light: Sunny.

Soil: Well drained, moist.

Fertilizer: 14-14-14 timed-release at planting, 5-10-5 thereafter.

Pruning: When the flowers fade, cut back the previous year's growth to new shoots already apparent.

Propagation: Take semiripe cuttings in summer.

Uses: Borders, specimen, screening, informal hedge, parks, background on large properties, bonsai.

WISTERIA
(wiss-TEER-ee-ah)

Wisteria

LEGUMINOSAE; pea family

Height/habit: Deciduous, woody, twining vines, 20–50 ft. (6–15 m.) long. Rigorous pruning can also produce a tree-form standard, 10–15 ft. (3–4.5 m.) high. Two fine types are Japanese wisteria (*W. floribunda*) and Chinese wisteria (*W. sinensis*).

Leaves: Compound, 13–19 leaflets, each to 3 in. (7.5 cm.) long.

Flowers: Single or double, pealike, in pendulous clusters, 1–1.5 ft. (30–45 cm.) long; purple, white, pink, red, or blue; fragrant; succeeded by dangling, velvety pods, 6–7 in. (15–17 cm.) long, lasting into winter.

Season: Primarily spring.

When to plant: Set transplants when available. Grafted plants known to have flowered are preferred to seed-grown or wild-harvested stock. Cold- and heat-tolerant zones 4–5 to 9.

Light: Sunny.

Soil: Well drained, moist.

Fertilizer: 14-14-14 initially, 5-10-5 subsequently.

Pruning: Cut back laterals to 5 or fewer leaflets in late summer, often again at early to midwinter; this encourages flowering spurs. In mild-climate gardens, wisteria often needs maintenance pruning on a biweekly basis in summer to control shape and size and encourage flowering.

Propagation: Sow seeds, take cuttings, layer, or graft in spring.

Uses: Cover for trellis, lattice, arbor, pergola, or fence; bonsai.

Chapter Three
Troubleshooting Guide for Woody Plants

Though generally easy to care for, woody plants sometimes experience problems. Here are some of the most common:

No blooms. Signals the need for more light, water, or fertilizer, and possibly more cold—lilacs, for example, require a certain number of hours of winter chilling; otherwise they will not bloom even though the plants may linger on for some years. Another possibility is that the plant needs more phosphorus (represented by the middle number in fertilizer NPK ratios, 15-30-15) and less nitrogen. Tree-form wisterias surrounded by a lawn that regularly gets a high-nitrogen fertilizer often do not bloom unless they are root-pruned or an area of turf is cut out around them equal to the branch spread; in this case, apply a low- or no-nitrogen fertilizer such as 1-6-5 or 0-6-5.

Insects clustered on new growth. Probably aphids, which often cluster on the tips of new shoots, especially after they have been given fertilizer with lots of available nitrogen. Wash off with strong streams of water; they will abate in due course, rarely causing permanent damage or requiring any serious pesticide treatment. Knock off with stiff streams of water from the hose. Can also be treated by spraying with insecticidal soap or Neem tree solution.

White or brown "bumpy" insects. Indicative of mealybugs or brown scale. Remove as many by hand as possible. Spray weekly and thoroughly with insecticidal soap, Neem tree solution, or horticultural oil.

Powdery white spots on leaves. Powdery mildew attacks some woody plants, especially crape myrtle early and lilacs late. Can be treated by applying fungicide or ignored. Crape myrtles often have powdery mildew early in the season (when nights are cool, days are warm). It is beneficial to treat them with a fungicide since the problem occurs early in their growth cycle; this is not needed for lilacs since they do not succumb to powdery mildew until they have done most of their work for the year.

Generally poor or weak growth. This indicates a need for more light, more water, and more nutrients. Avoid planting small shrubs where the soil is already laced with the roots of large trees. Ground covers can be established in these conditions, but first prepare pockets of cultivated soil.

Spider mites. Spider mites are often troublesome in hot, dry weather; spray under leafy shrubs and trees with strong streams of water. This discourages the mites.

Chapter Four
Bringing Woody Plants Into Your Home

Flowering and berry-covered branches make magnificent accents in the home. With a minimum of arranging, they add a note of drama to just about any room in the house, whether displayed in large floor vases or woven into swags and wreaths.

Woody cut branches remain fresher for a longer period of time if the lowermost inch (2.5 centimeter) or two is split with a knife or pounded with a mallet, then plunged immediately into deep water and left several hours or overnight to condition before being placed in a flower arrangement. Sometimes, branches look better if some or all of the leaves are stripped away, for example to reveal the wispy yellow flowers of fall witch hazel or the purple berries on a branch of callicarpa.

A most rewarding aspect of having one's own shrubbery border and garden with ornamental trees is that the branches of many can be cut during a winter warm spell, brought inside, and set to flower and leaf out early in vases of water. They last longest in cool, bright places, away from hot, direct sun rays and any currents from the heating system. Favorites include pussy willow, witch hazel, forsythia, flowering quince, flowering peach, flowering cherry, apple, crab apple, pear, flowering almond, lilac, and redbud.

Here are some other delightful ways to use woody plants indoors:

❧ Delicate flowers of spring-blooming trees and shrubs floated in decorative bowls of water, perhaps intermingled with votives

❧ Scarlet fall sassafras leaves with dried field grasses

❧ Yellow and orange fall ginkgo leaves with mountain ash berries

❧ Whole purple lilac blossoms in spring potpourri

❧ Fragrant petals of damask and cabbage roses or whole miniature roses in potpourri

The Art of Bonsai
Another facet of enjoying woody plants is training them in the ancient manner of Japanese bonsai, developed centuries earlier in China and known there as penjing. This can be a fascinating pursuit that leads the

practitioner to traveling in the Far East in search of visual images and hard goods—such as tools, trays, and pots—that help bring the art to life.

Bonsai, pronounced *bone-sigh* with even stress on both syllables, means literally "tray planting." The process involves root- and top-pruning to produce a dwarfed but vital plant. As practiced originally, the plants used were from moderate temperate climates; these types need moderate winter chilling, around 28°F (-2°C), in order to grow and flower radiantly. Since World War II, bonsai growers have embraced the vast flora of the tropics and subtropics, making it possible for apartment dwellers to grow bonsai successfully indoors year-round, in windows or under fluorescent lights.

Gardeners can also purchase bonsai in various stages of training. The plants range from months to centuries old. The only way to learn the art is to practice it, usually after observing a bonsai master at work. There are also well-illustrated manuals and videos covering all aspects of the pursuit. Local bonsai clubs are an ideal way to participate in this unique expression of art in the garden. Good candidates for miniaturization include maple, cedar, crab apple, and ginkgo.

The most fundamental law of bonsai is that the subjects are living and therefore require almost as devoted and consistent care as a household pet. This means daily or even twice-daily watering during the warmest, hottest seasons of the year.

Bonsai grow best and look their most picturesque if set on high tables or shelves outdoors. A traditional method is to stack concrete blocks on end for supports with 2-x-12-foot (61-x-360-centimeter) wood planks on top for sturdy shelving. You can also make garden display tables from wood or metal painted a mute or earthen color, in keeping with the hues of bonsai containers.

Bibliography

Bailey, Liberty Hyde, and Ethel Zoe Bailey; revised and expanded by the staff of the L.H. Bailey Hortorium. 1976. *Hortus Third*. New York: Macmillan Publishing Co.

Bailey, Ralph; McDonald, Elvin; Good Housekeeping Editors. 1972. *The Good Housekeeping Illustrated Encyclopedia of Gardening*. New York: Book Division, Hearst Magazines.

Graf, Alfred Byrd. 1992. *Hortica*. New Jersey: Roehrs Co.

Greenlee, John. 1992. *The Encyclopedia of Ornamental Grasses*. Pennsylvania: Rodale Press.

Heriteau, Jacqueline, and Charles B. Thomas. 1994. *Water Gardens*. Boston/New York: Houghton Mifflin Co.

Hobhouse, Penelope, and Elvin McDonald, Consulting Editors. 1994. *Gardens of the World: The Art & Practice of Gardening*. New York: Macmillan Publishing Co.

Hobhouse, Penelope. 1994. *On Gardening*. New York: Macmillan Publishing Co.

McDonald, Elvin. 1993. *The New Houseplant: Bringing the Garden Indoors*. New York: Macmillan Publishing Co.

McDonald, Elvin. 1995. *The Color Garden Series: Red, White, Blue, Yellow*. San Francisco: Collins Publishers.

McDonald, Elvin. 1995. *The Traditional Home Book of Roses*. Des Moines: Meredith Books.

Mulligan, William C. 1992. *The Adventurous Gardener's Sourcebook of Rare and Unusual Plants*. New York: Simon & Schuster.

Mulligan, William C. 1995. *The Lattice Gardener*. New York: Macmillan Publishing Co.

River Oaks Garden Club. 1989. Fourth Revised Edition. *A Garden Book for Houston*. Houston: Gulf Publishing Co.

Royal Horticultural Society, The; Clayton, John, revised by John Main. Third Edition. 1992. *Pruning Ornamental Shrubs*. London: Cassell Educational Ltd.

Scanniello, Stephen, and Tania Bayard. 1994 *Climbing Roses*. New York: Prentice Hall.

Schinz, Marina, and Gabrielle van Zuylen. 1991. *The Gardens of Russell Page*. New York: Stewart, Tabori & Chang.

Sedenko, Jerry. 1991. *The Butterfly Garden*. New York: Villard Books.

Sunset Books and Sunset Magazine. 1995. *Sunset Western Garden Book*. Menlo Park: Sunset Publishing Co.

Woods, Christopher. 1992. *Encyclopedia of Perennials*. New York: Facts On File, Inc.

Yang, Linda. 1995. *The City & Town Gardener: A Handbook for Planting Small Spaces and Containers*. New York: Random House.

Jacques Amand
P.O. Box 59001
Potomac, MD 20859
free catalog; all kinds of bulbs

Amaryllis, Inc.
P.O. Box 318
Baton Rouge, LA 70821
free list; hybrid Hippeastrum

Antique Rose Emporium
Rt. 5, Box 143
Brenham, TX 77833
catalog $5; old roses, also peren-
nials, ornamental grasses

Appalachian Gardens
Box 82
Waynesboro, PA 17268
catalog $2; uncommon
woodics

B & D Lilies
330 "P" St.
Port Townsend, WA 98368
catalog $3; garden lilies

The Banana Tree, Inc.
715 Northampton St.
Easton, PA 18042
catalog $3; seeds of exotics

Beaver Creek Nursery
7526 Pelleaux Rd.
Knoxville, TN 37938
catalog $1; uncommon
woodies

Kurt Bluemel
2740 Greene Lane
Baldwin, MD 21013
catalog $2; ornamental grasses,
perennials

Bluestone Perennials
7237 Middle Ridge
Madison, OH 44057
free catalog; perennials

Borboleta Gardens
15980 Canby Ave., Rt. 5
Faribault, MN 55021
catalog $3; bulbs, tubers,
corms, rhizomes

Bovees Nursery
1737 S.W. Coronado
Portland, OR 97219
catalog $2; uncommon
woodies

Brand Peony Farms
P.O. Box 842
St. Cloud, MN 56302
free catalog; peonies

Breck's
6523 N. Galena Rd.
Peoria, IL 61632
free catalog; all kinds
of bulbs

Briarwood Gardens
14 Gully Lane, R.F.D. 1
East Sandwich, MA 02537
list $1; azaleas,
rhododendrons

Brudy's Tropical Exotics
P.O. Box 820874
Houston, TX 77282
catalog $2; seeds,
plants of exotics

W. Atlee Burpee Co.
300 Park Ave.
Warminster, PA 18974
free catalog; seeds, plants,
bulbs, supplies, wide selection

Busse Gardens
5873 Oliver Ave., S.W.
Cokato, MN 55321
catalog $2; perennials

Camellia Forest Nursery
125 Carolina Forest
Chapel Hill, NC 27516
list $1; uncommon
woodies

Canyon Creek Nursery
3527 DIY Creek Rd.
Oroville, CA 95965
catalog $2; silver-leaved plants

Carroll Gardens
Box 310
Westminster, MD 21158
catalog $2; perennials,
woodies, herbs

Coastal Gardens
4611 Socastee Blvd.
Myrtle Beach, SC 29575
catalog $3; perennials

The Cummins Garden
22 Robertsville Rd.
Marlboro, NJ 07746
catalog $2; azaleas,
rhododendrons, woodies

The Daffodil Mart
Rt. 3, Box 794
Gloucester, VA 23061
list $1; Narcissus specialists,
other bulbs

Daylily World
P.O. Box 1612
Sanford, FL 32772
catalog $5; all kinds of
Hemerocallis

deJager Bulb Co.
Box 2010
So. Hamilton, MA 01982
free list; all kinds of bulbs

Tom Dodd's Rare Plants
9131 Holly St.
Semmes, AL 36575
list $1; trees, shrubs,
extremely select

Far North Gardens
16785 Harrison Rd.
Livonia, MI 48154
catalog $2; primulas,
other perennials

Flora Lan Nursery
9625 Northwest
Roy Forest Grove, OR 97116
free catalog; uncommon
woodies

Forest Farm
990 Tetherow Rd.
Williams, OR 97544-9599
catalog $3; uncommon
woodies in small sizes

Fox Hill Farm
P.O. Box 7
Parma, MI 49269
catalog $1; all kinds of herbs

Howard B. French
Box 565
Pittsfield, VT 05762
free catalog; bulbs

Gardens of the Blue Ridge
Box 10
Pineola, NC 28662
catalog $3; wildflowers
and ferns

D. S. George Nurseries
2515 Penfield Rd.
Fairport, NY 14450
free catalog; clematis

Girard Nurseries
Box 428
Geneva, OH 44041
free catalog; uncommon
woodies

Glasshouse Works
Greenhouses
Church St., Box 97
Stewart, OH 45778
catalog $2; exotics for
containers

Gossler Farms Nursery
1200 Weaver Rd.
Springfield, OR 97477
list $2; uncommon
woodies

Greenlee Ornamental Grasses
301 E. Franklin Ave.
Pomona, CA 91766
catalog $5; native and
ornamental grasses

Greer Gardens
1280 Goodpasture Island Rd.
Eugene, OR 97401
catalog $3; uncommon
woodies, especially
Rhododendron

Grigsby Cactus Gardens
2354 Bella Vista Dr.
Vista, CA 92084
catalog $2; cacti and
other succulents

Growers Service Co.
10118 Crouse Rd.
Hartland, MI 48353
list $1; all kinds of bulbs

Heirloom Old Garden Roses
24062 N.E. Riverside Dr.
St. Paul, OR 97137
catalog $5; old garden, English,
and winter-hardy roses

Holbrook Farm and Nursery
Box 368
Fletcher, NC 28732
free catalog; woodies and
other select plants

J. L. Hudson, Seedsman
P.O. Box 1058
Redwood City, CA 94064
catalog $1; nonhybrid flowers,
vegetables

Jackson and Perkins
1 Rose Lane
Medford, OR 97501
free catalog; roses, perennials

Kartuz Greenhouses
1408 Sunset Dr.
Vista, CA 92083
catalog $2; exotics
for containers

Klehm Nursery
Rt. 5, Box 197 Penny Rd.
So. Barrington, IL 60010
catalog $5; peonies,
Hemerocallis, hostas,
perennials

M. & J. Kristick
155 Mockingbird Rd.
Wellsville, PA 17365
free catalog; conifers

Lamb Nurseries
Rt. 1, Box 460B
Long Beach, WA 98631
catalog $1; perennials

Las Pilitas Nursery
Star Rt., Box 23
Santa Margarita, CA 93453
catalog $6; California natives

Lauray of Salisbury
432 Undermountain Rd.
Rt. 41
Salisbury, CT 06068
catalog $2; exotics
for containers

Lilypons Water Gardens
6800 Lilypons Rd.
P.O. Box 10
Buckeystown, MD 21717
catalog $5; aquatics

Limerock Ornamental Grasses
R.D. 1, Box 111
Port Matilda, PA 16870
list $3

Logee's Greenhouses
141 North St.
Danielson, CT 06239
catalog $3; exotics for
containers

Louisiana Nursery
Rt. 7, Box 43
Opelousas, LA 70570
catalogs $3–$6;
uncommon woodies,
perennials

Lowe's Own Root Roses
6 Sheffield Rd.
Nashua, NH 03062
list $5; old roses

McClure & Zimmerman
Box 368
Friesland, WI 53935
free catalog; all kinds of bulbs

Mellinger's
2310 W. South Range Rd. North
Lima, OH 44452
free catalog; all kinds of plants

Merry Gardens
Upper Mechanic St., Box 595
Camden, ME 04843
catalog $2; herbs,
pelargoniums, cultivars
of Hedera helix

Milaeger's Gardens
4838 Douglas Ave.
Racine, WI 53402
catalog $1; perennials

Moore Miniature Roses
2519 E. Noble Ave.
Visalia, CA 93292
catalog $1; all kinds of
miniature roses

Niche Gardens
1111 Dawson Rd.
Chapel Hill, NC 27516
catalog $3; perennials

Nichols Garden Nursery
1190 N. Pacific Highway
Albany, OR 97321
free catalog; uncommon
edibles, flowers, herbs

Nor'East Miniature Roses
Box 307
Rowley, MA 01969
free catalog

North Carolina State University
Arboretum
Box 7609
Raleigh, NC 27695
Propagation guide for woody
plants and lists of plants in
the arboretum, $10; member-
ship permits participation in
worthy plant propagation
and dissemination.

Oakes Daylilies
8204 Monday Rd.
Corryton, TN 37721
free catalog; all kinds
of Hemerocallis

Geo. W. Park Seed Co.
Box 31
Greenwood, SC 29747
free catalog; all kinds of seeds,
plants, and bulbs

Plants of the Southwest
Agua Fria, Rt. 6,
Box 11A
Santa Fe, NM 87501
catalog $3.50

Roses of Yesterday and Today
802 Brown's Valley Rd.
Watsonville, CA 95076
catalog $3 third class,
$5 first; old roses

Roslyn Nursery
211 Burrs Lane
Dix Hills, NY 11746
catalog $3; woodies, perennials

John Scheepers, Inc.
P.O. Box 700
Bantam, CT 06750
free catalog; all kinds of bulbs

Seymour's Selected Seeds
P.O. Box 1346
Sussex, VA 23884-0346
free catalog; English
cottage garden seeds

Shady Oaks Nursery
112 10th Ave. S.E.
Waseca, MN 56093
catalog $2.50; hostas, ferns,
wildflowers, shrubs

Siskiyou Rare Plant Nursery
2825 Cummings Rd.
Medford, OR 97501
catalog $2; alpines

Anthony J. Skittone
1415 Eucalyptus
San Francisco, CA 94132
catalog $2; unusual bulbs,
especially from South Africa

Sonoma Horticultural Nursery
3970 Azalea Ave.
Sebastopol, CA 95472
catalog $2; azaleas,
rhododendrons

Spring Hill Nurseries
110 W. Elm St.
Tipp City, OH 45371
free catalog; perennials,
woodies, roses

Sunnybrook Farms Homestead
9448 Mayfield Rd.
Chesterland, OH 44026
catalog $2; perennials, herbs

Surry Gardens
P.O. Box 145
Surry, ME 04684
free list; perennials, vines,
grasses, wild garden

Terrapin Springs Nursery
Box 7454
Tifton, GA 31793
list $1; uncommon
woodies

Thompson & Morgan
Box 1308
Jackson, NJ 08527
free catalog; all kinds
of seeds

Transplant Nursery
1586 Parkertown Rd.
Lavonia, GA 30553
catalog $1; azaleas,
rhododendrons

Twombly Nursery, Inc.
163 Barn Hill Rd.
Monroe, CT 06468
list $4; uncommon
woodies

Van Engelen, Inc.
Stillbrook Farm
313 Maple St.
Litchfield, CT 06759
free catalog; all kinds
of bulbs

Andre Viette Farm & Nursery
Rt. 1, Box 16
Fishersville, VA 22939
catalog $3; perennials,
ornamental grasses

Washington Evergreen Nursery
Box 388
Leicester, NC 28748
catalog $2; conifers

Wayside Gardens
One Garden Lane
Hodges, SC 29695
free catalog; all kinds
of bulbs, woodies,
perennials, vines

We-Du Nursery
Rt. 5, Box 724
Marion, NC 28752
catalog $2; uncommon
woodies, perennials

White Flower Farm
Box 50
Litchfield, CT 06759
catalog $5; woodies,
perennials, bulbs

Whitman Farms
3995 Gibson Rd., N.W.
Salem, OR 97304
catalog $1; woodies,
edibles

Gilbert H. Wild and Son, Inc.
Sarcoxie, MO 64862
catalog $3; perennials, peonies,
iris, Hemerocallis

Winterthur Plant Shop
Winterthur, DE 19735
free list; uncommon woodies

Woodlanders
1128 Colleton Ave.
Aiken, SC 29801
catalog $2; woodies,
hardy Passiflora

Yucca Do
P.O. Box 655
Waller, TX 77484
catalog $3; woodies, perennials

Credits

Special thanks to these gardeners and institutions where I photographed the trees and other woody plants chosen for this book:

Stanley and Gunvor Adelfang, Huntsville, AL

American Horticultural Society, River Farm, Alexandria, VA

Ernesta and Fred Ballard, Philadelphia, PA

Barnsley House, Rosemary Verey, Gloucestershire, England

British Columbia, University of, Botanic Garden, Vancouver, BC

Brooklyn Botanic Garden, Brooklyn, NY

Francis Cabot, La Malbaie, Quebec

Central Park, New York, NY

Great Dixter Gardens, England

Thomas Dodd Nurseries, Semmes, AL

Mr. and Mrs. Duncan Pitney, NJ

C. Z. Guest, Old Westbury, NY

Hickey-Robertson, The Farm, Nelsonville, TX

Hidcote Manor Gardens, Gloucestershire, England

Jardins des Plantes, Paris, France

Joe Kirkpatrick, Memphis, TN

Leonardslee Gardens, England

Logee's Greenhouses, Danielson, CT

Longwood Gardens, Kennett Square, PA

Bonny and David Martin, Memphis, TN

Mercer Arboretum and Botanic Gardens, Humble, TX

Mohonk Mountain House, New Paltz, NY

Moody Gardens, Galveston, TX

Georgia and Eugene Mosier, Sewickley Heights, PA

National Wildflower Research Center, Austin, TX

The New York Botanical Garden, Bronx, NY

Mr. and Mrs. Dave Pendarvis, Lake Charles, LA

Geo. W. Park Seed Co., Inc., Greenwood, SC

Planting Fields Arboretum, Oyster Bay, NY

Mrs. J. Pancoast Reath, PA

Virginia Robinson Gardens, Beverly Hills, CA

Royal Botanical Gardens at Kew, London, England

Victor Salmones, Acapulco, Mexico

Sissinghurst Castle Gardens, Kent, England

Susan Turner, Baton Rouge, LA

Upton House Gardens, England

Wakehurst Gardens, England

William T. Wheeler, New York, NY

Index

U.S.D.A. *Plant Hardiness Zone Map*

Average Annual Minimum Temperature

Temperature (°C)	Zone	Temperature (°F)
-45.6 and below	1	below -50
-45.6 and -45.5	2a	-45 to -50
-40.0 to -42.7	2b	-40 to -45
-37.3 to -40.0	3a	-35 to -40
-34.5 to -37.2	3b	-30 to -35
-31.7 to -34.4	4a	-25 to -30
-28.9 to -31.6	4b	-20 to -25
-26.2 to -28.8	5a	-15 to -20
-23.4 to -26.1	5b	-10 to -15
-20.6 to -23.3	6a	-5 to -10
-17.8 to -20.5	6b	0 to -5
-15.0 to -17.7	7a	5 to 0
-12.3 to -15.0	7b	10 to 5
-9.5 to -12.2	8a	15 to 10
-6.7 to -9.4	8b	20 to 15
-3.9 to -6.6	9a	25 to 20
-1.2 to -3.8	9b	30 to 25
1.6 to -1.1	10a	35 to 30
4.4 to 1.7	10b	40 to 45
4.5 and above	11	40 and above

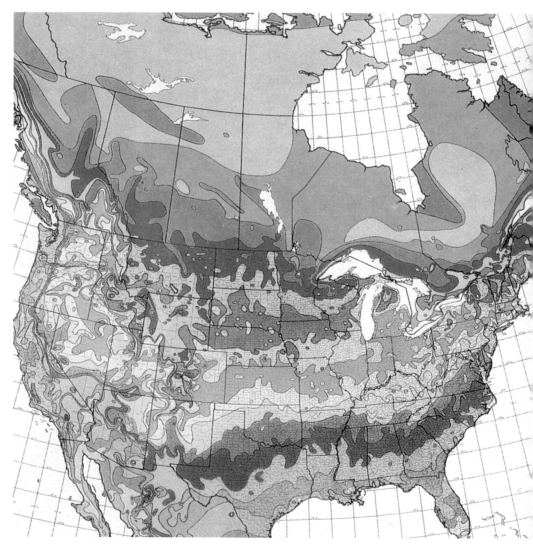

This map, issued by the United States Department of Agriculture, lists average annual minimum temperatures for each zone. It relates directly to the cold-hardiness of plants, but does not address the other extreme, high temperatures. Special considerations with regard to these matters are noted as appropriate throughout the pages of this book.
A new map, in preparation by the U.S.D.A. in cooperation with the American Horticultural Society, will treat equally matters of hot and cold and their effect on plants.